Biblical
Manhood
AND
Womanhood

Aubrey Malphurs

kregel
PUBLICATIONS

Grand Rapids, MI 49501

Biblical Manhood and Womanhood: Understanding Masculinity and Femininity from God's Perspective

Copyright © 1996 by Aubrey Malphurs

Published by Kregel Resources, an imprint of Kregel Publications, P.O. Box 2607, Grand Rapids, MI 49501. Kregel Resources provides timely and relevant resources for Christian life and service. Your comments and suggestions are valued.

Cover design: Alan G. Hartman
Book design: Nicholas G. Richardson

Library of Congress Cataloging-in-Publication Data
Malphurs, Aubrey.
   Biblical manhood and womanhood: understanding masculinity and femininity from God's perspective / Aubrey Malphurs.
     p.   cm.
   Includes bibliographical references.
   1. Women—Biblical teaching. 2. Men—Biblical teaching. 3. Marriage—Biblical Teaching. 4. Bible. O.T. Genesis I–III—Commentaries 5. Bible. N.T. Ephesians V—Commentaries I. Malphurs, Susan. II. Title
BS680.W7M35   1996   261.8'343—dc20   96-31497
                                              CIP

ISBN 0-8254-3195-6

Printed in the United States of America
1 2 3 4 5 / 00 99 98 97 96

I'm especially indebted to my wife, Susan, who has not only participated in this effort but has supported it with patience and constructive criticism.

Contents

Introduction

R andy Brown grew up in the 1970s in a dysfunctional home located somewhere in blue-collar East Dallas, Texas. His mom worked steadily as a bookkeeper with a small insurance firm in the heart of downtown Dallas. Her stable job held life and limb together since they couldn't count on his father's erratic income to provide for their family of four. Randy's dad was a small-time contractor who struggled from one job to the next. Most important and memorable in Randy's young life was that his dad was an alcoholic.

When Randy thinks back to those early, difficult years, he remembers that Dad was either away working late hours in an attempt to finish some remodeling job for an upset customer, or he was slumped in his recliner in front of the television with a beer in one hand and a cigarette in the other. As he watched the smoke from the cigarette curl up to the ceiling and disappear, Randy would quietly swear to himself, "I'll never grow up to be like that!" While to an outsider the situation may have appeared harmless—only an exhausted dad relaxing before supper—it was a precursor to the hard whiskey that anesthetized his dad's constant pain and supposedly empowered him to survive the nightmare that had become his life.

Randy remembers that as a small child he used to lie in bed awake at nights, frightened and worrying if they would make it. It seemed as though his mom and dad fought all the time. Mom resented being the bread winner in the family because Dad's work was so sporadic. He managed to get some jobs but promptly lost them. People refused to wait several weeks for him to complete work that should have taken a few days at most. One week they would hire him, and the next week they would fire him and find someone else. He would start a job and

7

then disappear for days. Later, Randy or his mom would find him in a local bar where he'd spent the advance he'd been given for his next remodeling job. Randy recalls that most of the phone calls he answered back then were from irate customers trying to locate his dad, or anxious bill collectors demanding to speak with either his mom or dad.

Randy filled the vacuum in his life with athletics. They provided a route of escape from his many disappointments at home; they enabled him to focus on something else. Even at the young age of five, he was playing soccer with the older kids in the neighborhood, and he was quite good at it. In elementary school he added baseball, basketball, and football to his sports repertoire. When it came to choosing up sides for a game, the teams considered Randy a high draft pick—he always went first or second. His prestige as a natural athlete not only made him feel good about himself, but also built up a protective wall that insulated him from the gnawing pain he felt when he allowed himself to think about how bad things were at home.

While Dad was usually too busy to spend any time with him, he did come to some of Randy's games. Like Randy, his dad had been a good high-school athlete and had played one year of semi-pro baseball in Florida's Grapefruit League. He viewed his dad as his distant fan, proudly sitting somewhere alone up in the bleachers critiquing his every move. He knew that Dad believed in him and even admired him, yet he needed more, much more from a man. Mom was equally unavailable. She was at work all day and then came home to make supper and prepare Randy and his brother for bed. After she tucked them in, she washed several batches of laundry, attempted to clean the house, and ceaselessly nagged his father who was too distant emotionally to even try to defend himself.

Randy graduated from high school and made all-state in baseball and soccer. He was promptly rewarded with a baseball scholarship to Southern Methodist University in Dallas. SMU was not known for its baseball team, but Randy wanted to stay near his home. He felt that it was the least he could do to help his mother, who had gotten all of them through the tough times. His dad eventually died due to heart complications, leaving behind a stack of unpaid bills. Mom didn't make much money, but she doggedly kept at it, working lots of overtime until she eventually paid off their debt. This alleviated much of the stress and gave them some room to breath financially.

Meanwhile, Randy's brother, Robert, had become a problem.

Robert struggled academically and emotionally through grade school and promptly dropped out of high school. Early in life they had been close, very close. Both had been there for one another, and Robert still seemed to hold respect for and even listened on occasion to, Randy's advice. Randy had to be strong for this family, and his brother in particular.

* * *

Carol Jones grew up with her mother in a single-parent home in the somewhat modest suburban community of Richardson, Texas, just north of Dallas. While her mother and father split up and went their separate ways shortly after her fourth birthday, her dad had emotionally abandoned his wife even before Carol was born. He had traded their relationship for his position as the marketing director for a large firm, Maxus Energy Corporation, located in Los Colinas near the new Dallas-Fort Worth Airport.

During the first year of the divorce, Mr. Jones spent time with Carol on a regular basis. Like clockwork, he was there each month to take her to a nice restaurant and then a movie. She really looked forward to those times with her dad. He made her feel important—like she was somebody special. Secretly, down deep, she hoped against hope that somehow her mom and dad would get back together, and they could be a family again. In fact, that desire was the main ingredient in her prayers to God.

Then her dad met Sharon, a woman at work, who was several years younger and more attractive than her mom. That meant he had less time for Carol. She began to realize that things were different when he uncharacteristically began to call at the last minute and cancel their special dates together. Something always seemed to come up. Carol first met Sharon when Dad brought Carol along on some of their dates. The realization that her dad had found, and was serious about, someone else had a crushing effect on Carol. He pretended to be interested in her, but it wasn't the same—he couldn't take his eyes off Sharon. Then Carol's hope evaporated when her dad announced that he was going to marry Sharon. Carol was crushed. While little Carol smiled on the outside, she wept on the inside. Why had God disappointed her? Why had God allowed this to happen?

Within a few months, after a quiet wedding, her dad and his new bride had all but dropped out of her life. She saw him sporadically throughout the following year, but he never seemed to have much time for her. Sharon demanded his time and attention, and she would not share him with anyone, including Carol. He showed up for her birthdays wearing a big smile and carrying some special present, but he was not the same. He seemed detached and aloof. The following year he was not able to make her birthday—Sharon explained that he was out of town on business. Carol felt her dad slipping through her little fingers, and she could do nothing about it but cry.

Her response to her disappointment was to blame her mom for not being able to keep her dad. Mom had failed both him and her. But mostly she blamed herself. What was wrong with her? Why didn't her daddy love her anymore? What had she done to drive him away? She thought he loved her. What had begun as a special relationship between a little girl and her dad had turned into a casual, but painful, relationship. She clung to her memories and desperately sought to push the intruding pain of her present situation out of her life. She hoped against hope that she was still her daddy's little girl—that was all she had to hold on to from her childhood. It would have been too painful to acknowledge the truth. She learned to anesthetize her quiet, chronic pain by taking control of the things in her life—take charge of your own life, she thought, and then no one can hurt you.

Carol was an excellent student. During her high school years she excelled in academics and was awarded an all-expense-paid scholarship to Southern Methodist University in Dallas. She really didn't need it since her dad wanted to pay for everything. She wondered if it made him feel better about their relationship—or lack of one. Her mom had also found success as the vice president of news programming with a television station in Dallas. Regardless, Carol relied on the scholarship and declined help from either of her parents. It made her feel good—real good—to be on her own, to be in charge of her own life.

It was while she was at the university that Carol met Randy. They did not meet on campus but at Fellowship Community Church, a contemporary evangelical church located near the university. Randy's roommate also attended SMU on a baseball scholarship and had become a Christian through the ministry of Campus Crusade. He invited Randy to some of the meetings, and eventually, after numerous discussions that lasted until the early hours of the morning, Randy trusted in the Savior. Randy had some real problems with the idea of God, especially as father. He felt very distant from God, as if God had abandoned him somewhere in the past. Randy and his roommate had begun to attend Fellowship Community Church when they weren't away for baseball games.

Carol's roommate was a Christian and invited her to church. Carol believed that she might have come to know Christ at a very early time in her life; perhaps it was at a vacation Bible school sponsored by the Baptist church that she and her mom sporadically attended after her mom's divorce. That would account for what she felt had always been a belief in God and an awareness of his presence in her life. Regardless, she and her roommate began to regularly attend Fellowship Community Church. They both enjoyed the contemporary worship and the singles ministry, and it was at the latter that she met Randy Brown.

The relationship had been rather casual at first. They did not date but somehow managed to meet and sit together during the meetings. In time they found that they were attracted to one another and began to date on a steady basis. They explained to both of their roommates that they were just good friends, but both knew better. Something unexplainable seemed to be drawing them together.

Randy wondered, Am I really in love with Carol? He had dated occasionally throughout high school but experienced no serious relationships. His love was sports, not women. In his quieter, thoughtful moments, however, he admitted (at least to himself) that he had a real fear of girls. He feared that even though he was competent at athletics he would not prove competent in relationships, especially deep relationships, particularly relationships with the opposite sex. At this point in his life, his roommate was the closest friend he had ever had other than his brother. He carried a deep fear that once people, especially girls, got to know him, they would uncover his relational naiveté, his sense of incompetence, and reject him. The safest stance for Randy was to avoid any entanglements with the opposite sex and to concentrate instead on what he knew best, which was sports.

But Carol proved to be different. She sensed his relational struggle but somehow seemed to make it easy for him to relate to her. Perhaps she knew what it meant to feel all alone. When he was around her, he didn't feel so lonely anymore. She wasn't like other girls he had dated, and he was strongly attracted to this woman. He needed her, and she seemed to need and enjoy his presence. She made him feel competent around her.

But where was this relationship headed? Randy found himself lying awake at night, asking this and numerous other questions. He had once overheard his aunt tell his mother that he, not his dad, was the real man in the family. That was difficult for his young ears to hear because he had struggled to view his dad as a man. Except for an occasional coach, his dad was the best example of a man that he had in life, and he desperately needed a model, flawed as it was. Whereas athletics made Randy feel more like a real man, Carol made him really feel like one. That was extremely important to him. What was going on inside him? What did it mean to be a man, an authentic man? What was he all about, not just in terms of his past, but his present, and in particular, his sexuality? Carol had stirred something deep within him, and he was eager to find out more even though it might prove painful.

Carol was experiencing similar feelings toward Randy. While she had dated in high school, her daddy had been the only man in her life until Randy came along. She felt things when she was with Randy that she had only felt as a little girl with her dad. Was this a part of growing up and becoming a woman? These stirrings attracted her to Randy, but deep down, it frightened her. Where was this relationship going? She was strongly attracted to him. Maybe she even loved him— she was not sure. But what if this relationship led to marriage? Would Randy marry her only to leave her as her father had so many years ago? She didn't believe that she could survive another abandonment. Could she as a woman trust him as a man? Could she risk vulnerability? Would she only be disappointed again?

Randy's presence in Carol's life was stirring up feelings and memories that she thought she had put behind her. She was not sure what it was like to be a woman because no one had ever treated her as a real woman—not even her dad, who, after divorcing Sharon, still occasionally popped up in her life. She wasn't even sure what a real woman was. Initially, Carol felt that her dad really loved her, but later she knew within that it wasn't true. He had only disappointed and abandoned her as he had her mom, Sharon, and eventually a third wife. She had never felt truly loved by anybody. Though her mom was around, she was not there for Carol—she was too busy pursuing her own career that served to dull the deep, abiding pain over losing her husband, a pain that she couldn't seem to escape. Carol had been wounded deeply. She felt no strong emotional attachment to anyone. Instead a sense of low self-worth hung like a dark cloud over her head. Could she be the woman in Randy's life? What did it mean to be a woman, that is, the real thing—an authentic woman? What was her sexuality all about? She had believed that part of being a modern woman was taking charge of her own life—being in complete control. That way no one could hurt her ever again. Where had that need to control come from? Was there room for Randy? Could she control him? She suspected that her mom had tried to control her dad, especially as the marriage unraveled, with disastrous results. Would she and Randy experience the same? Most important, they both had accepted Christ, and He had taken a very prominent place in their lives. What difference did Christianity make? What difference would or could Christ make in their relationship? They were both very confused.

* * *

All across America many people like Randy and Carol, baby boomers and baby busters, are asking the same questions that Randy and Carol are asking about their sexuality. The issues in question surfaced with the women's movement in the 1960s and 1970s and have been compounded and somewhat confused by the corresponding men's movement in the 1980s. Christian boomers and busters are asking the same questions of themselves. They are looking for some answers—some real answers—to their questions about their sexuality. What is sexuality? Is there a biblical sexuality? What does it mean to be an authentic man or an authentic woman? Does the Bible have anything to say about human sexuality? While Christian women have asked these questions much longer, Christian men have also begun to ask some hard questions and probe their sexuality as evidenced by the explosion of, and tremendous response to, the ministry of Promise Keepers.

What is most exciting for the cause of Christ and His church is that many men and women are turning to Christianity and the Scriptures for the answers to the tough questions posed by human sexuality. While they may have found some relief from a secular psychological and sociological approach, they want answers based on the truth of Scripture. They desire to know what God has built into a woman and a man. Perhaps this seeking is God's way of initiating a spiritual revival across a post-Christian North American landscape that now sees 80 to 85 percent of its churches plateaued or in decline.

I approach the topic of sexuality not from a distance as a casual spectator, but from up close, real close, as a participator, a fellow-participator in search of his own sexual identity. To a great extent the information in this book is a vital part of my own pilgrimage in life. It represents an attempt to discover my own manhood—what it means for me to be a real man. Like Randy I grew up with an alcoholic father and a faithful mother who worked constantly to hold our small family together.

But what is human sexuality? Is this a book about physical sex? Many people hear the term "sex" and think that sexuality is all about physical relationships. Some uninformed people view the Bible as a prudish book when it comes to the topic of physical sex. They naively view it as no more than the product of a group of prim Victorian ladies who wrote for some remote audience. While the Bible was not written as a manual on the physical aspects of sex, it does have something vital and relevant to say about the topic (read Song of Solomon in the Old Testament for a surprisingly frank description in poetic form of love relationships).

The physical aspects of sexuality, however, are not the focus of this book. A major emphasis of this work, and I believe of the Bible, is that there is a significant difference between human sex and human sexuality. The former has to do with a very beautiful, intimate physical act designed by God for two loving, married adults. While the latter, sexuality, may include sex, it is much bigger and addresses the natural differences between a man and a woman that are at the very core of their being. Sexuality has everything to do with what it means to be a man or woman. It captures our entire personhoods as male and female; it is at the very heart of how we express ourselves in relationship to one another. It's important to understand at the beginning how I see the meaning of human sexuality throughout this book, and that I'll be using it this context from cover to cover.[1]

What does the Bible have to say about maleness and femaleness? What does it have to tell us about the essence of human sexuality? Will it give us a clearer sense of our femininity and masculinity? I don't think that the Bible was intended as an explicit primer on human sexuality. I'm convinced, however, that it does have much to say about the topic, especially in Genesis 1–3 in the Old Testament and Ephesians 5 in the New Testament. Genesis 1–3 is foundational to the rest of the Bible on the topic of womanhood and manhood. That's where it all began. Adam and Eve wrestled with their sexuality much as we do today. Ephesians 5 complements and adds commentary on Genesis 1–3. The issue is not so much where but what—what are these passages saying about what it means to be a man and a woman? What do they tell us that would help us to understand first our own sexuality and then that of another such as a girlfriend, a boyfriend, or our spouse?

It is also important and fascinating to note that most of these passages view human sexuality—maleness and femaleness—not separately but side by side. The Scriptures place them in context with one another. In Genesis 1–3, Adam as a man is understood best in relation to Eve as a woman. The same is true in the New Testament. This in no way diminishes singleness (Paul recommends it in 1 Corinthians 7) but suggests that womanhood and manhood are best understood in context with one another. It is impossible to understand one without the other. Something vital would be missing. Maleness is understood best in light of how it complements—and contrasts with—femaleness, and vice versa.

Genesis 1–3 and Ephesians 5 address human sexuality from the perspective of marriage. Adam and Eve are husband and wife. Ephesians 5:22–33 is addressed to wives and husbands. These portions of Scripture, however, have much to say to singles as well as marrieds. Scripture will help single men and women understand themselves and the opposite sex. For example, when we examine the results of Adam's and Eve's first act of disobedience to God in Genesis 3 (what theologians call "the Fall"), we'll discover that God's judgment on Eve was that she would attempt to take over, or control, Adam. The judgments in Genesis 3, however, go beyond Adam and Eve and affect us all. Consequently, not only will Eve desire to control Adam, but women will have a desire to control men—whether a spouse, fiance, boyfriend, boss, employee, or some other man.

In this book I'll use certain biblical terms such as *dominance*, *head*, and *submission*. These have become real turnoffs for many women, and some men, because their misuse has resulted in much misunderstanding, abuse, and false teaching on biblical sexuality. Throughout history, some have twisted the first two concepts of dominance and head to sanction the abuse and domination of women. I would ask that the readers, especially those who react adversely to these terms, withhold judgment until we've studied them in their proper biblical contexts. Scripture clearly distinguishes between male dominion that resulted from the Fall in Genesis 3 and headship that originated in Genesis 2. These two must not be confused in any way.

The third term, *submission*, is also broadly misunderstood. The New Testament uses it in terms of a woman's response to her husband. One common misconception in Christian circles is that submission means a woman is the passive partner in a dominant-passive relationship. Another is that she's a doormat—someone that her husband can walk all over at will. Neither, however, is accurate, as we'll discover in chapters 6 and 7. False teaching on male headship and the woman's submission has caused much emotional, and sometimes physical, abuse of women. I hope that the biblical approach of this book will help to remedy this situation.

Where do a man and a woman come up with their concepts of manhood and womanhood? I believe that they originated with the first human couple—Adam and Eve. We still bear at the very core of our being their imprint, genetic and otherwise, which explains much of human sexuality, whether in the first century or the twenty-first century. What happened to them in the Garden was a precursor that explains much of what takes place in the life of a contemporary man and a woman such as a Carol or a Randy.

In addition to our distant great-grandparents, Adam and Eve, our human parents have much to do with our view of sexuality. Little girls such as Carol learn what it is like to be a woman from both their moms and dads. Moms model womanhood and dads complement it by treating and valuing their daughters as females. Little boys also learn what it means to be a man from their dads and moms. They want to grow up to be men just like their dads, a view balanced by the response of their moms. The glaring problem in contemporary America is that there aren't many fathers around for little boys to model after. They are either physically or emotionally absent and thus not available. Consequently, many boys grow up in single-parent homes, modeling after their mom or some neighborhood hero. The lack of a father's presence, physically or emotionally, has just as devastating an effect on little girls, as demonstrated by Carol's relationship to her dad. When a young boy and girl enter adolescence, however, many look beyond their parents for clues to their sexual identity. Most imbibe deeply from their culture. In particular, young men and women are deeply influenced by their heroes, usually famous male and female sports personalities, rock stars, Hollywood actors and actresses, a local gang, and others.

A major problem with looking to the culture to define and determine our sexuality is that modern popular culture is so fickle—it's constantly changing. Hollywood has demonstrated this well over the years in terms of manhood. In the 1950s, John Wayne represented the man's man. He was a warrior—a tough, virile, don't-dare-let-'em-see-you-cry kind of person who was polite to, but felt extremely awkward around, women. This image changed in the 1960s with men such as Hugh Hefner and James Bond, who not only were tough and virile, but also slick and sexy with women. These movie images served to degrade women, often portraying them as little more than mindless sex objects or, in a more contemporary term, as "bimbos."

In the 1970s, however, there was a decided shift to a man's "softer side." Actors such as Alan Alda and Woody Allen portrayed men who weren't so tough—men who were more sensitive and somewhat introspective. The message was "Men, get in touch with your inner feelings!" Then all this changed again in the 1980s when actors such as Arnold Schwarzenegger and Sylvester Stallone hit the box office. They represented men as both tough, smart, and very competitive. Finally, the 1970s man and the 1980s man combine to form the "Neo Man" of the 1990s, who is both sensitive and in touch with his emotions while strong, tough, and smart. Perhaps the epitome of this is Arnold Schwarznegger's role in the film *Kindergarten Cop*.

The male who allows his culture to define and dictate his sexuality will soon become as confused as a chameleon in a paint store. Whereas from the 1960s to the 1980s the concept of manhood changed about every decade, in the 1990s it's changing much faster. Males who take their cues from the culture find themselves not only confused, but frustrated and exasperated. They are asking such questions as, Who am I? How do I relate to the opposite sex? What do they expect from me? And it is the same for women as well? Confusion reigns.

What is needed is a view of sexuality that is true, timeless, and

authentic. I'm convinced that we can only find such a view in the
Scriptures. The Bible addresses our sexuality in a way that is both
accurate and relevant, and with an aura of authenticity. No single
passage of Scripture explicitly defines or conveys human sexuality.
You can't look in the index of your Bible and find a section entitled
"Biblical Sexuality." Instead, we'll examine the passages in Genesis
1–3 and Ephesians 5.

This book has three major parts. The first is "The Creation of Human
Sexuality" and presents God's original design and intent for a couple
such as Randy and Carol as male and female. The first chapter examines
Genesis 1 and God's creation of the man and the woman as equals in
his image to co rule creation. The second chapter studies Genesis 2
and God's establishment of the man as the responsible, serving leader
and the woman as his supportive helper. This is a complementary
relationship that God designed to bring maximum fulfillment spiritually,
emotionally, and physically to both the woman and the man.

The second part is entitled "The Corruption of Human Sexuality."
While Genesis 1 and 2 do not represent the real world as experienced
by boomers and busters like Carol and Randy, Genesis 3 is the real
world—the world in which men and women live and relate to one
another as male and female. This section of the book explains what
went wrong. Chapter 3 presents Satan's temptation of the man and
woman and explains how they violated their sexuality, which led to
their disobedience. Chapter 4 covers the Fall and the consequences
of Adam and Eve's disobedience as it affected their intimacy with
God and one another. Chapter 5 presents God's judgments on Satan,
the man, and the woman, and its devastating impact on all humanity.

The third part of the book is entitled "The Redemption of Human
Sexuality." As we transition to the New Testament, we discover the
difference that Christianity makes in our sexuality. We see what
happens when Christ enters the picture. We discover the difference
that He can make and what a redemptive relationship looks like
between a man and a woman. Chapter 6 describes God's redemptive
design for the woman in Ephesians 5:22–24, and chapter 7 describes
his complementary design for the man in Ephesians 5:25–33.

I have provided a list of questions at the end of each chapter to
help you to think through the issues and apply the biblical contents of
each chapter to your life. These questions are for both single and
married women and men.

Notes

1. Some would refer to this as "gender" and not sexuality. They use sex and sexuality in the same context of biological differences and use gender of the other differences between men and women.

PART I

The Creation of Human Sexuality

The first two chapters of Genesis present God's original design and intent for Adam and Eve, human sexuality, and ultimately for Randy and Carol. In Genesis 1 God creates the man and the woman as equals in his image. In Genesis 2 God establishes the man as the serving leader and the woman as the supporting helper in a complementary relationship that brings both maximum fulfillment spiritually, emotionally, and physically.

1

The Equality of Human Sexuality
Equal Image-Bearers

Randy and Carol, as a single male and female, are asking the hard but critical questions that confront human sexuality. Randy asks, What does it mean to be an authentic man? Early in life he looked to his dad and then to sports for the answer to his question. While he found answers, they were fleeting at best. His dad proved more a disappointment than a model of human masculinity. Displaying a maturity beyond his years, Randy recognized that sports would be short-lived and diminish in impact as he grew older. While he worked hard at being the best shortstop he could be, he had discovered that his involvement in baseball had not brought him a richer understanding of what it means to be a man. What would happen to his feelings of manhood when he could no longer play baseball?

Carol asks, What does it mean to be an authentic woman? For a brief time as a little girl, she had looked to her dad for the answer to the question. That had proved devastating. Not only had he failed her, but he had left her wondering what was wrong with her. She discovered that the passing of time and sporadic dates with various guys had not accomplished any healing nor provided additional insight. It seemed that whenever a guy became interested in her and began to move toward her relationally, she shifted into hyper-control and ran them off. Men resented her self-protective, I'm-in-charge approach, and stiff-armed her, moving toward other, safer relationships.

As Christians, both Carol and Randy need and want clear personal concepts of their sexuality. They are looking for real answers that

will give them a greater understanding of who they are as a man and
a woman and an appreciation for their distinctiveness. Only the Bible
provides the real answers to these questions. Unlike their personal
experiences that were interlaced with disappointments, the Scriptures
provide significant answers that not only are true but are timeless and
thus always relevant.

The biblical teaching on human sexuality begins with the creation
of sexuality in Genesis 1 and 2. These early chapters are critical
because they provide the very foundation upon which a concept of
human sexuality is built, as well as the foundation of other biblical
texts on the same. The story unfolds in two dramatic acts. Act 1 is
Genesis 1. The camera views this dramatic scene from a distance,
and we see the creation as a whole. Moses, the writer, gives us the
big, all-inclusive picture of what took place at creation. The message
in Genesis 1 is that God created the man and woman, human sexuality,
in his image. This first act consists of two scenes.

SCENE 1: GOD CREATES HUMAN SEXUALITY

In the first scene of Act 1, God creates the man and the woman,
Adam and Eve. The creation story does not begin, however, with the
creation of human sexuality. Instead, we see God as Creator enmeshed
in the entire creative process.

The Creation of Creation

The origin of life remains for most scientists and philosophers the
major unsolved problem of all prior human history. Whatever the age
of the earth, men have been trying to unravel the mystery of how life
began as far back as the earliest recorded history. At the end of the
twentieth century, however, standard science remains baffled over a
solution to the mystery. It seems the more man learns the less he
knows. All the various views and theories of the origin of life have
served not to enlighten, but to deepen the mystery.

In the 1950s when Elvis ruled rock 'n' roll and Ike Eisenhower
was President, Dr. Stanley Miller, a scientist and researcher, was sure
that he was close to an answer. Working in a University of Chicago
laboratory, Dr. Miller believed that with a simple apparatus he had
been able to generate some of the crucial building blocks of life. He
filled a flask with boiling water and certain gases (ammonia, methane,
and hydrogen) believed to be present in the earth's atmosphere when

life began. Then he exposed the contents of the flask to several generated electrical sparks designed to simulate the effects of lightning. After a week the contents of the flask turned "deep red and turbid." Miller found dissolved in this primordial soup certain amino acids that are the basic components to the building blocks of life.

Men and women need a clear,
personal concept of their sexuality.

This experiment and others like it provided the foundation for modern research into the origin of life and the major theories that prevail at the end of the twentieth century. The only problem is that four decades later, Dr. Miller and others are no closer to the answer than in the 1950s. Scientists now believe that the earth's atmosphere contained different gases, that lightning was not the probable catalyst, and that life formed in a freezer, not in a boiling flask.

What we've learned from science regarding the origin of life is that we don't learn from science. What is assumed to be true in theory at one point is later overturned by one new theory after another. For science, the origin of life remains elusive. All current theories of life's origin rest more on the plausible arguments of men than on the hard facts of scientific evidence.

God has saved man much time and needless speculation by explaining the origin of life in Genesis 1 and 2. As long as science and philosophy choose to disregard the Genesis account, then they will continue to dabble in first one theory and then another—this is destined to be the future of origin-of-life research.

Genesis 1:1 says that God created the heavens and the earth. It is God who created creation. That's how the earth was given birth. He didn't, however, begin with the man and the woman. Genesis 1:2 states that the earth was formless and empty. Before God created Adam and Eve, He first formed and filled the earth in preparation for them.[1] I believe that had we been there, the power of the Creator and the beauty of his creation would have overwhelmed us. It must have been an awesome display of his creative power and beauty. Every time I watch a Texas sunrise or sunset, it reminds me of creation. Yet the scintillating mixtures of the various shades of color are only a mere hint of, a brief glimpse, at what was present at creation.

On the first three days of creation, God formed the earth. On day one, He created light in the midst of darkness, bringing about night and day. On day two, He created the sky that served as an atmospheric expanse to separate the waters that formed the clouds from the waters below. On day three, He created land that produced various plants or bushes, and fruit trees.

Over the next three days, God filled what he had formed. On day four, God made the sun, the moon, and the stars to fill the expanse He created on day two and to govern day and night to serve as signs to mark the seasons and to give light for the earth. On day five, He created all the species of water life to fill the water below, and He spoke and created various species of birds to fill the air. On day six, God created all species of animals to live on the earth.

The Climax of Creation

All of this builds, however, to a striking climax—the man and the woman on day six. It's as if God saved the best until last. He created the man and the woman separately from the rest of creation in general, and the animals in particular. The creation was building to a great crescendo. Adam and Eve are special. He created creation for himself and for them, and He created them to rule over (Gen. 1:28) and enjoy (Gen. 2:8, 9) his creation.

Up to this point in the creation account, the writer has said nothing about the gender of the birds, animals, or water life. He makes a point, however, of stating in Genesis 1:27 that Adam and Eve are male and female. The point is that gender is not as important for the other creatures as it is with the man and the woman. He has created human sexuality—manhood and womanhood. That is who they are; that is their identity.

SCENE 2: GOD CREATES
HUMAN SEXUALITY IN HIS IMAGE

In the second scene of Act 1 we discover that more is taking place on the sixth day than the creation of human sexuality. Not only is the creation of man a special event, but Genesis 1 says that God created the man and the woman in his image. Genesis 1:26 specifically states: "Let us make man in our image, in our likeness. . . ." And Genesis 1:27 concludes: "So God created man in his own image, in the image of God he created him. . . ."

The Man and Woman Are God's Image-Bearers

The image of God addresses the essence of our sexuality. It has to do with the very core of our being. God did not create any of the other creatures—the animals, birds, or water life—in his image. Ortlund writes: "Man is unique, finding his identity upward in God and not downward in the animals."[2] This was something special for the man and woman alone that they didn't share with anyone or anything else. God created human sexuality to reflect his image. Adam and Eve were image-bearers. Manhood and womanhood, biblically understood, are by creation a reflection of God's image.

But what does this mean? What does it mean to say that God created the man and woman in his image? The answer in part is found in the context—the verses that follow.

They Can Produce Life. First, God created the man and woman in his image so that just as God produced life, so they can produce life. Genesis 1:28 says that: "God blessed them and said to them, 'Be fruitful and increase in number; fill the earth. . . .'" Thus a part of God's blessing for them was the ability to procreate other living beings. In bringing life into this world, Adam and Eve mirrored God. Child-bearing in the Bible was very important both to husbands and their wives. Women in the Old Testament who experienced infertility, such as Sarah (Gen. 11:30, 16:1) and Rachel (Gen. 30:1), experienced extreme anguish over their condition—they considered themselves cursed of God. They would resort to great extremes to provide a child for their husbands (Gen. 16:1–2; 30:3).

In bringing life into this world,
Adam and Eve mirrored God.

Couples who experience infertility feel much the same anguish and heartbreak today. In my discussions with them, I have discovered that many unconsciously fear that their inability reflects on their very sexuality—that a man in his inability to procreate somehow feels less a man, and a woman in her inability to conceive, carry, and deliver a baby feels less a woman. Being able to bear children reflects God's image as Creator and affects us at the very core of our sexuality.

They Have Dominion over Creation. Second, God created man
and woman in his image so that as He has dominion over the world,
they have dominion over the world. Genesis 1:28 says: "God blessed
them and said to them, 'Be fruitful and increase in number; fill the
earth and subdue it. Rule over the fish of the sea and the birds of the
air and over every living creature that moves on the ground.'"

The divine purpose and destiny of human sexuality was to rule the
world. This means that God originally intended for Adam and Eve to
have control over his creation here on earth. Ross believes that the
terms used here in part suggest putting down opposition and anticipate
the coming conflict with evil.[3] Regardless, the man and the woman—
human sexuality—would be in control of the world that God had so
carefully prepared for them. Human sexuality has much to do with
control. Later, sin will interfere and the man and the woman will turn
on one another, attempting to control one another (Gen. 3:16c). In
our contemporary world, some have labeled this the battle of the sexes.

They Share God's Character. Third, God created human sexuality
in his image so that Adam and Eve shared many of his attributes.
True, God is unique in many ways. He is all-knowing in that He knows
everything there is or could be (Ps. 147:4). Our knowledge is finite.
He is everywhere present in this universe though separate from it (Ps.
139:7–12). Although our schedules sometimes mistakenly place us
in different locales at the same time, we can be in only one place.
God is all-powerful (Rev. 19:6), whereas, our power is greatly limited
in numerous ways. God also never changes (Mal. 3:6). He was the
same yesterday as He is today and will be tomorrow. We, however,
find ourselves in a state of constant change, physically, emotionally,
and spiritually.

Adam and Eve mirrored God's character
to one another. These qualities express what it was
like to be in a relationship with each other.

But God created human sexuality to have many attributes in
common with Himself. These include such character qualities as
sensitivity, integrity, strength, tenderness, caring, unconditional love,

honesty, faithfulness, patience, kindness, gentleness, authenticity, forgiveness, approachability, and so on. If you had been present, you would have observed and experienced these qualities in Adam and Eve. We weren't present, however, which raises the question, To whom did they mirror these attributes?

First, they reflected them to God. When God saw Adam and Eve and fellowshipped with them, He saw and experienced Himself as reflected in them. They loved Him with no strings attached; they were honest, caring, and faithful to Him as He was to them.

Second, they mirrored these fine attributes to one another. These qualities express what it was like for them to be in a relationship with one another and were essential to their sexuality. Adam and Eve were sensitive to one another, acted with integrity, were tender, caring, and loved one another unconditionally. They experienced authenticity, gentleness, and were always approachable. I believe that these are vital character qualities affecting our human sexuality today. Every man and woman longs for these qualities in his or her spouse and enter into relationships expecting to find them. Perhaps this expectation is traceable in some way back to the Garden. While men and women rarely see these qualities consistently expressed in the relationships of most other couples, they hope against hope that their relationship will be different, that they will treat one another in this manner.

Both the Man and the Woman Reflect God's Image

God created both the man and the woman in his image. He didn't include the man and exclude the woman. Genesis 1:27 says: "God created man in his own image, in the image of God he created him; *male and female he created them*" (italics mine). The divine image rested separately and equally on both of them, and Adam later passed the image on to his son Seth (Gen. 5:1–3). Confusion might exist in the mind of some readers because verse 27 uses the term "man" for Adam and Eve. Most likely the author of Genesis uses the term either generically or to anticipate the man's responsibility in the man-woman relationship of Genesis 2.[4] Regardless, the last few words clarify that both the man and the woman will mirror his image.

What's the point? God in his infinite wisdom makes it clear that the man and the woman are equal in essence. This passage hints strongly at the essential equality of the sexes—that God values both and that both are of equal worth in the eyes of God. Nowhere does Scripture teach male superiority or female inferiority. This passage teaches that manhood and womanhood are co-equal in the image of God and would seem to include all men and women (non-Christians) regardless of their relationship to Christ. In Galatians 3: 28, Paul adds that men and women (Christians) are also equal in Christ. He writes: "There is neither Jew nor Greek, slave nor free, male nor female, for you are all one in Christ Jesus."

God in His infinite wisdom makes it clear that the man and the woman are equal in essence. They are both of equal worth in the eyes of God.

Why is biblically-stated equality so important? While I'm not aware of any prominent Christian leader or spokesperson who teaches that men are essentially superior to women, it doesn't lessen the fact that some men, Christian as well as non-Christian, often consider women as essentially inferior. This attitude manifests itself most often in some form of abuse.

At present in America the focus is primarily on physical abuse. In fact, the problem has grown to such an extent that in March of 1995, President Clinton appointed a former Iowa Attorney General, Bonnie Campbell, to head a government task force to bring an end to physical violence against women. The violent crime of rape illustrates the scope of the problem. Most are aware of America's rising crime rate. The president of the American Medical Association argues that there exists an epidemic of violence in the Untied States. Noting that the homicide rate alone is far above that of any other country, he states, "We do live probably in the most violent country on the face of the earth."[5] The incidence of rape, however, is rising at three times the crime rate.

The primary place of abuse is in the home. According to President Clinton, domestic violence in the United States is the number-one health risk for women between the ages of 15 to 44.[6] It poses a bigger threat than either cancer or car accidents. The FBI estimates that a woman is beaten an average of once every twelve seconds. And most often when the spouse is beaten, the children are beaten as well. Until recently, most have looked at domestic violence as a purely private matter. With the passage of the domestic violence provisions of the anti-crime law by Congress in 1994, the federal government has gotten into the act. It hopes to partner with health professionals, social workers, local police officers, and prosecutors in enforcing the new law. Senator Joseph Biden, a Democrat from Delaware, sums up the new thrust: "This is a major step forward in putting everyone on notice that we are finally taking violence against women seriously."[7]

I'm convinced that a major part of the problem of violence against women is pornography. It's no respecter of persons, adding to the destruction of individuals from serial killer Ted Bundy to television evangelist Jimmy Swaggert. Often women are not aware that pornography demeans them in the worst way. Men who imbibe deeply in pornography acknowledge that they view women as an inferior gender who are in this world exclusively to serve them and their needs. Much contemporary pornography highlights the so-called joys of sadomasochistic sex, simulated and real rape, and the whipping, bondage, and torture of women. When you catch a glimpse of the true content of hard-core pornography, it's not hard to believe the many researchers and studies that confirm its contribution to the abuse and degradation of womanhood. Consequently, Christian men who have been under the influence of pornographic material such as magazines, movies, and videos for any lengthy period of time will tend to devalue women. Therefore, it's imperative that they seek professional help, especially before they consider marriage.

If physical violence against women
is reaching epidemic proportions, then emotional
violence is a raging epidemic.

Obviously physical abuse against women has become a major problem in America. Emotional abuse, however, most often precedes and accompanies physical abuse. While a man may have never struck his wife physically, every man consciously or unconsciously has emotionally abused his wife, and wives their husbands. If physical violence against women is reaching epidemic proportions, then emotional violence is a raging epidemic. Again, where there is emotional abuse of wives, there is emotional abuse of children. In most situations, this sin affects the entire family.

Some may question the federal government's involvement in violence, especially domestic violence, against women and doubt its ability to enforce the laws it makes. Regardless, it's time that the church in general, and Christian men in particular, deal with this problem. It's totally naive to believe that some Christian men don't have a problem with pornography and the physical abuse of women. Not only must we deal with the problem within our Christian ranks, but we as men must speak out against this abuse. We have discovered in Genesis 1 that men are not essentially superior to women. God created both in His image and values both equally. Therefore, Christians, and Christian men in particular, must set the example for the watching world all around us. This is an important part of our responsibility as salt and light to a lost and dying generation (Matt. 5:13–14).

We must value and honor one another as men and women created in the image of God. This means that Christian men should value not only their wives, but other women, both Christians and non-Christians alike. The believing man must honor his wife as a fellow image-bearer and set the example for his family at home. Similarly, he must also value women in the church and in the marketplace as image-bearers, including those who have authority over him, his peers, and those who work for him. Valuing women involves not only treating them as fellow image-bearers but requires men to reflect God's image in their relationship with women.

An example is when a man listens to a woman whether she is his boss, peer, wife, daughter, mother, secretary, or functioning in some other role. Everyone, female as well as male, wants to be heard. Some men will not consider the contributions of a woman because she is a woman. This is tragic because a man shows deep respect when he listens to a woman and genuinely respects her opinions regardless the topic. Listening to a woman sends her the message that not only what she is saying is important but that she is important as a person.

All the above applies to women as well. While the male gender has been notorious for abuse toward women, it can easily work the other way. Feminism has helped women across North America gain some of their basic human rights such as the right to vote. Extreme feminism (hard-core feminism), however, has encouraged women to oppose and rebel against men in general and has gone so far as to embrace lesbianism. Militant feminism only complicates the problem and further alienates women and men. Consequently, both genders must relate not as adversaries but as illuminaries, or those who mirror the very image of God. That's an important part of what it means to be an authentic man or woman. Men and women should see in one another such character qualities as sensitivity, integrity, tenderness, trust, honesty, patience, kindness, authenticity, and approachability.

DISCUSSION QUESTIONS

For Men

1. Who's the most prominent female that you relate to at present (girlfriend, wife, mother, daughter, boss, peer, employee, other)?

2. What are some things that you can do to honor or value her as a person created in God's image?

3. Your assignment is to honor this person within the next day or two or as soon as possible. Once you have done this, answer the rest of the questions below.

4. What did you do to value this person? How did she respond? Were you surprised? Why or why not? Will you do this again and/or something else to honor her? Why or why not?

For Women

1. Who's the most prominent male that you relate to at present (boyfriend, husband, father, son, boss, peer, employee, other)?

2. What are some things that you can do to honor or value him as a person created in the image of God?

3. Your assignment is to honor this person within the next day or two or as soon as possible. Once you have done this, answer the rest of the questions below.

4. What did you do to value this person? How did he respond? Were you surprised? Why or why not? Will you do this again and/or something else to honor him? Why or why not?

Notes

1. Allen P. Ross, *Creation & Blessing: A Guide to the Study and Exposition of Genesis* (Grand Rapids: Baker Book House, 1988), p. 104.

2. Raymond C. Ortlund, Jr., "Male-Female Equality and Male Headship: Genesis 1–3" in *Recovering Biblical Manhood & Womanhood*, ed. John Piper and Wayne Grudem (Wheaton, Ill.: Crossway Books, 1991), p. 96.

3. Ross, *Creation & Blessing*, p. 113.

4. Ortlund, "Male–Female Equality," p. 98.

5. Laura Beil, "AMA leader asks for war on violence," *The Dallas Morning News*, April 14, 1995, p. 28A.

6. Kathy Lewis, "Clinton acts to stop attacks on women," *The Dallas Morning News*, March 22, 1995, p. 1A.

7. Ibid., p. 20A.

2

The Functions of Human Sexuality
Complementary Partners

What initially had been a safe, casual relationship between Randy and Carol was becoming serious and complex. At first, their paths seem to cross unintentionally and mostly at church. Now they admittedly looked for ways to spend time with each other almost every day, whether on campus or at Fellowship Church. Several months before they had both agreed to stop dating other people. She was constantly on his mind and vice versa. What had begun at a snail's pace was now a roaring freight train. Where was this relationship headed? Because of their strong commitment to Christianity, they believed that it was wrong to live together. Randy considered it only for a fleeting moment before moving on to the thought of marriage. For them cohabitation was not a viable option.

Complex thoughts and feelings that lurked deep within both of them seemed to work their way to the surface during their more quiet, reflective moments when they were apart. These emotions served to balance the feelings they stirred in one another and the attraction each felt for the other. For Randy the villain was always the same, the intense and uncontrollable fear of not knowing how to really relate to a woman. He believed (as best he knew how) that what he felt inside toward Carol was love. But once committed to love, would it only be a matter of time before his feelings of incompetence found a way to destroy their relationship? To think about it was terribly painful and difficult. It brought back the memories of those early, difficult years, and the many disappointments and the ominous feeling of inadequacy he encountered growing up in a dysfunctional family. He realized that somewhere within he feared love because he dreaded that it might be snatched away.

Carol felt herself propelled, almost mercilessly at times, by the gnawing guilt that somehow her dad's divorcing her mom and abandoning their family was her fault. Maybe somehow she could have prevented it had she been a better daughter. From girlhood to early womanhood, through the perceived safety of academics, she had fought unsuccessfully another, even more tragic demon: the numbing, terror of abandonment that began with her dad's early demonstration of how quickly love could evaporate. The moment real love was near, the sheer fear that it might again be brutally ripped from her rose from her soul to engulf her like a raging current. Though she had come to understand the cause of her fear, the emotion was still difficult for her to control. It was always much easier to control the source of the emotion. In the past, the source was an occasional, interested young man; now it was Randy.

Wisely, they both began seeing a Christian counselor who was on staff at Fellowship Community Church. As he attempted to help them uncover and work through their personal problems, he also led them in a study of biblical womanhood and manhood to help them arrive at a personal concept of their sexuality. In Genesis 1 they studied that God created the man and woman in his image; consequently, they were of equal value in his eyes. This was not a problem for Randy since he highly respected his mom for all she had done in working and keeping their family together in spite of his father's alcoholism. He extended this respect to most other women. He felt some distrust, however, of those in the feminist camp. Carol was convinced that his feelings were a carryover from his early involvement in male-dominated sports.

Carol struggled more with this teaching because of her exposure to several strongly feminist professors at the university. On the one hand, she felt some anger toward men, perhaps her dad, who devalued and treated women poorly, while on the other hand, she struggled with her own feelings of low self-worth due to her dad's abandonment. She worked hard, however, and with the counselor's constant probing, her understanding of God's view of her worth, and Randy's help, she experienced significant healing and growth.

They both needed much help in their responsibilities toward one another as a man and woman—especially in the context of marriage. Whenever their counselor probed this area, red flags popped up and furiously waved until they had everyone's attention. With the potential for a more permanent relationship in mind, Randy had begun to ask, What would be my relationship to Carol as her husband? What are my responsibilities in a marriage relationship? He was a traditionalist at heart and believed in marriage for life, not "until divorce do us part." Carol had already begun to ask similar questions regarding herself several months before Randy's sudden inquisitiveness.

Scripture addresses these questions and others in Genesis 2. The message of Genesis 1 is that God created manhood and womanhood in his image. Genesis 2 adds that he created them to complete one another. Thus, the message of Genesis 1 and 2 is that God created human sexuality in his image to complete one another. Whereas Genesis 1 was Act 1, Genesis 2 provides both the content and the context for Act 2 of God's creation drama. In Act 1, the camera disclosed the entire panorama of creation from a distance so that we see the big picture. In Act 2, however, the camera moves in tight for a closer look. And rather than focusing on all of God's creation, it narrows to his creation of the man and woman.

In Act 2, the creation account returns to the creation of human sexuality and provides us with more information of what took place. In Genesis 2, God creates both the man and the woman in His image for a purpose—to relate to one another. But what is their relationship and how are they, as well as Carol and Randy, to accomplish it?

GOD DESIGNED THE MAN AND WOMAN TO COMPLETE ONE ANOTHER

God Created Adam First

Genesis 1:26–27 simply states that God created the man and the woman. We might assume from Genesis 1 that God created womanhood and manhood at the same time. In Genesis 2:7, however, we discover that God created Adam before He created Eve. The order is important, and I'll return to it later in this chapter. Verse 7 indicates that God created and fashioned Adam "from the dust of the ground." So Adam begins his existence before Eve as a somewhat frail, earthy creature in comparison to the sovereign God who is his Creator.

Nonetheless, he and all who would come after him, man or woman,

were also created with dignity in God's image and are of eternal worth
to God. In Mark 8:36–37, Jesus says that a human life is worth more
than all the wealth and possessions of this world. In Matthew, Jesus
elevates humanity far above the rest of creation, including plants (Matt.
6:30), birds (Matt. 6:25–26; 10:29–31), and sheep (Matt. 12:12). With
the inbreathing of life, man became a living soul, capable of a
relationship with his Creator.

We find in the rest of this section in Genesis that God had
significantly blessed Adam. In short—he had it made! First, God
placed him in a perfect environment—he lived in Paradise (vv. 8–
10). There God provided him with trees that were not only pleasing
aesthetically, but supplied him with food. Most important, he enjoyed
and experienced God's presence (Gen. 3:8). Second, God gave him a
perfect employment. The point is, work is good and a part of God's
purpose and plan for man (Gen. 2:5). Adam not only lived in
Paradise—he took care of Paradise (vv. 5 and 15) and worshiped and
served his God there.[1] I suspect that as Adam worked and cared for
the Garden of Eden, he experienced a strong sense of significance
and fulfillment that what he was doing with his life really counted for
something important. This is work as God originally intended it. God's
purpose was that man's work would be a blessing not a burden. Adam's
life and work had a profound sense of purpose—he was serving and
worshiping his Creator.

God Created Adam Alone

We find, however, a startling contrast of mood in Genesis 2:18.
The author reveals that though Adam had it all, he was all alone. God
created man incomplete. There was a gaping void in his life—
something or someone was missing. Man cannot live by job alone!
He was relationally incomplete. He was not yet all that God intended
for him to be. Adam must have become acutely aware of his loneliness
when God paraded all the animals by him for names, and yet none
was able to fill the emptiness in his soul. This implies that manhood
is experienced most fully in the presence of womanhood, and vice
versa. Adam was discovering that he would best realize and express
his maleness when completed by femaleness, and vice versa.

I suspect that this relational emptiness is what we feel when single.
Like a visitor, it invades our lives about the time of puberty but remains
until death. It's that which gives us a thirst for a significant relationship

with the opposite sex, and it's that which attracted Randy and Carol to one another. While there is absolutely nothing wrong with being single (Jesus and Paul were single), many singles feel and struggle with emptiness, especially as they reach their thirties and forties. They must keep in mind, though, that Paul commends singleness and views it as freeing up a person for greater service to Christ (1 Cor. 7:25–38). He also warns that marriage has its struggles and can be very painful: "But those who marry will face many problems in this life, and I want to spare you this" (1 Cor. 7:28).

Adam was relationaly incomplete. He was not yet all that God intended him to be.

God, however, moves to fill the void in Adam's life—to supply what is missing. In verses 21–22, he creates Eve. She's the missing ingredient in His recipe for life. Commenting on the creation of Eve, Paul writes in 1 Corinthians 11:9 that she was created for Adam. This does not, however, imply that she was in any way inferior to him. The point is that God created her to complement him, for in verses 11–12 Paul teaches that they are mutually dependent. In verse 11 he writes: "In the Lord, however, woman is not independent of man, nor is man independent of woman." God created man and woman not mutually independent but collectively dependent. Paul's point is that they need one another. Both bring something to the relationship that benefits the other. Their relationship is one of interdependence. They are to be complementary partners.

The reasoning behind his point is in verse 12: "For as woman came from man, so also man is born of woman." Paul alludes to God's creation of Eve from Adam's rib. Thus, initially the woman came from the man. But that does not mean that he is superior to her because Paul adds that ever since, men have come into this world through women—their mothers. First Corinthians 11:11–12 teaches that theirs is to be a complementary relationship. God created them to complement each other.

But what might that look like? If we clothed the concept with flesh, what would we see? In an article *in The Dallas Morning News,* Steve Kinny writes about a couple, Michelle DeBosier and Brian Hickey, who had much in common throughout life. Their families were from

New York; they went to high school in North Dallas; they attended the same college. After graduation, they returned to live in Dallas, Texas, attended the same church, knew all the same people, and liked many of the same things—athletics, biking, and camping. But, they weren't able to make that special connection. The problem was that every time they ran into one another, she was on a date. Finally he got up enough nerve to ask her out. It was only a month later that they agreed to stop dating other people. Soon thereafter they decided to get married. At the end of the article, Brian expresses feelings for Michelle that illustrate well what Adam must have felt after God brought Eve to him. Kinny writes, "Brian says Michelle has made him 'a more complete person. Michelle gave me something I had been looking for,' he says. 'There's no comparison from the person I was before I met her.'"[2]

Randy could say much the same in his feelings for Carol, and they aren't married yet. As two people begin to come together, there seems to be an inborn sense that they are completing one another, the expectation that after marriage they will not be the same as before, that both will benefit mutually from their oneness. Randy will recognize and express his maleness best in the presence of Carol. Carol will experience and enjoy her femaleness most fully in the presence of Randy.

GOD DESIGNED THE MAN AND WOMAN
TO COMPLETE ONE ANOTHER DIFFERENTLY

While Adam and Eve both had the same purpose, to complement each other, God designed them as a team to accomplish that purpose, but differently. Adam and Eve were a community. Although God designed them to serve together as partners on the same team, they were also different. Before the Fall their differences helped primarily to complete one another and were at the core of their sexuality. Since the Fall, those differences have often worked to divide more than complement. (Again, Paul warns of the problems couples will face in marriage in 1 Corinthians 11:28.)

Certain contemporary voices, however, argue that outside the female and male anatomy, a man and woman are essentially the same. In a 1995 ABC special entitled "Men, Women, and the Sex Difference," host John Stossel interviewed Bella Abzug and Gloria Steinem. Both argued that the only essential difference between men and women is our anatomy, and while it is true that boys and girls and men and women behave differently, those differences are caused by socialization, not creation—we are bred differently, not born different.

Other voices, however, from the world of science quietly say men and women are different. They argue that those differences start in the womb; we are biologically wired to be different. New technologies designed to catch the mind in the very act of thinking show that men and women use their brains differently.[3] For example, men retain a sense of direction better than women, while women have a better memory for detail. Women also tend to have better language skills, whereas men tend to have better math skills. Men see things in three dimensions, while women hear better and are more sensitive to people's emotions.

> *Other voices from the world of science quietly say that men and women are biologically wired to be different.*

Scripture teaches that men and women differ more than just anatomically, biologically, or socially. While they have similarities, God designed and designated that men and women function in different roles. Though essentially equal, they work uniquely. These differences serve to help men and women complement and not duplicate each other's efforts in serving God. Scripture distinguishes two overarching functions for men and women in community.

GOD DESIGNED ADAM TO BE THE PRIMARY LEADER IN THEIR RELATIONSHIP

You won't find the term "head" anywhere in Genesis 1–3. To the contemporary female who lives in the long shadow cast by the women's movement of the 1960s and 1970s and feels the strong influence of feminism in the 1980s and 1990s, the term may sound somewhat harsh. It's a biblical term, however, that goes back to the first century. Paul uses it in 1 Corinthians 11 to describe a man's responsibility for his relationship with his wife in the first century and ultimately the twenty-first century. Paul's intent was that the concept behind "head" be functionally and spiritually liberating, not exasperating, for women. In 1 Corinthians 11:3 he writes that: "the head of the woman is man." His point is that the man is responsible for his wife. Therefore, he argues in verses 5–7 that the woman (wife) should honor her head (her husband). In the culture of the first century, one way that women honored their husbands in church was by wearing some kind of head covering.

> *Paul's intent was that the concept behind the term "head" be functionally and spiritually liberating, not exasperating, for women*

The basis for Paul's position is found in 1 Corinthians 11:8–9 where he argues from the creation and purpose of Eve in Genesis 2. He writes: "For man did not come from the woman, but woman from man; neither was man created for woman, but woman for man." Verse 8 is a clear reference to the creation of Eve in Genesis 2:21–23. Verse 9 is a reference to Eve's purpose as stated in Genesis 2:18. While Adam is not called the head in Genesis 2, Paul obviously understood this chapter as distinguishing the function of the man from the woman, and that Adam was in effect the responsible head of their relationship, Paul doesn't want anyone to misunderstand, however, that while the man is to function as the head, this doesn't mean that his wife is inferior to him. So he adds a comment to this effect in verses 11–12.

Other events appear to announce that God put the primary responsibility for their relationship in Adam's hands. One event was Adam's naming of Eve (Gen. 2:23; 3:20). The act of naming is an exercise of dominion that God granted to Adam as co-ruler of creation. Thus, Adam gave names to all the livestock, birds, and beasts (Gen. 3:19, 20). Adam's naming of Eve, however, was different because she was his equal, not an animal. His naming of Eve was an act of headship not dominion.[4]

Another event in Genesis 3 that signaled male responsibility took place after the Fall. When Eve ate of the forbidden fruit, her eyes were not opened immediately. But when Adam ate, both their eyes were opened and both became aware of what they had done (v. 7). In addition, both heard God walking in the garden and both hid from God (v. 8), but God addressed the rest of the conversation up to the judgments to Adam (vv. 9–11). Adam was the leader in their relationship and the responsible party for that relationship.

What all this means is that God holds the husband responsible for his wife and family much as the stockholders hold a CEO responsible for a corporation. Manhood involves responsibility. That doesn't mean that God blames the husband when a wife or some other family member rebels against God, unless the man has contributed in some way to that rebellion. This does, however, send a strong message to men who avoid their responsibilities as husbands and parents. The tendency for men in the second half of the twentieth century is not to lead and be spiritually strong in their families. Far too many are emotionally and spiritually impotent and opt, instead, to literally abandon their families for various reasons that aren't legitimate (work, another woman, sex, and so on). A classic example is Carol's dad, who abandoned her and her mom at a very fragile time in Carol's young life.

But what does it mean for the man to be the head of the relationship? The term itself means authority; it's the authority to lead. This is its meaning as it appears in most other places in the New Testament (Eph. 1:22; 4:15; 5:23; Col. 1:18; 2:10, 19). But authority has a twin called responsibility. Wherever there is authority, there is also responsibility. But that authority and responsibility must always be in balance. The more authority you have, the more responsibility you must take. The more responsibility you have, the more authority you need to properly exercise that responsibility. God has given the authority and thus the responsibility for leadership in the family to the man.

The point is that when two or more people partner together for any reason (ministry, family, employment), one must be the primary leader who has the authority to lead and takes responsibility for the relationship. That's why a ship has only one captain, and an airplane has only one pilot who is the captain. Can you see them in a dire emergency (the ship is sinking or the plane's engines have stalled), frantically attempting to convene a committee to reach a decision about what to do? This doesn't mean that a leader doesn't consult with others and get their opinions. That's essential to good leadership. People, however, have an innate need to know "where the buck stops." We want to know who the responsible party is, to whom do we look for leadership? I'm aware of several situations where two men have attempted to co-pastor a church. It has rarely worked, if at all. In fact, several pastors who have attempted a co-pastorate have asked me to give their phone numbers to others who might be considering a co-pastorate so that they can talk them out of it. Co-leadership has proven to be no leadership. It has proven to be leadership by compromise not consensus.

God has given the authority and thus the responsibility for leadership in the family to the man.

We discover in 1 Corinthians 11:3 that the equal members of the Trinity also minister with a primary leader to accomplish their purpose. Paul writes that God the Father, though equal with God the Son, is the head of the Son. God, in effect, is the point person in the Trinity. It doesn't mean that He never consults with the other members, or that He leads as a despot. It does mean that He's proactive, not passive, in the relationship; He leads and takes responsibility for his decisions. If the most perfect relationship in existence operates this way, then certainly we should not have a problem operating similarly. We would be wise to learn from it.

In a marriage relationship, God has given the man the authority to be the point person. He has designated him as the primary, responsible leader. And this is based on design, not superiority of gender. Designation is based on design. Not only has God uniquely designed each of us individually, but He has designed men differently from women. God originally designed and thus designated the man to function as the responsible leader in his relationship with his wife. I suspect that this creative design is a part of what took place in Genesis 2:7. God built into Adam all that he needed to be a natural leader. Before the Fall there was within Adam an innate predisposition to lead. Otherwise, God wouldn't have designated him as leader. God would not ask the man to do what he wasn't capable of doing. This is why sexuality includes male and female functions, or roles. These roles intuitively grow out of who a man or women is by nature. Eve and Adam functioned a certain way because God designed them to do so.

As the responsible head or leader, the man relates in numerous ways to his wife. I have placed just a few of these in a subset under the term "leader" (fig. 1). This subset consists of such functions as service, initiative, protection, involvement, strength, decisiveness, as well as others.

THE MAN AS PRIMARY LEADER

**He serves, initiates,
protects, provides,
involves, is strong, decides, etc.**

(Figure 1)

I have purposely used the term "primary" to describe the functions of both the man and the woman. I don't believe Scripture completely restricts these roles to gender. I'm using these functions as primarily, but not exclusively designated to, the male or female. A man's primary responsibility is to lead, that is, to serve, protect, provide, be strong, and decide. That doesn't mean that there aren't times when a women may serve, protect, provide, show strength, and so on.

Servanthood

According to the New Testament, a primary component of biblical leadership is servanthood. But what does that mean? And what does it mean for a man to serve his wife, fiancee, or girlfriend?

Christ gives us some insight into what it means to be a servant leader in Matthew 20:25–28. In verse 25, he first explains what it isn't: "You know that the rulers of the Gentiles lord it over them, and their high officials exercise authority over them." Here he contrasts servant leadership with a dominating style of leadership exercised by Gentiles or pagans. His point is that servant leaders aren't to dominate, use, and abuse their followers. They aren't to be tyrants. While a leader may have authority over others, that doesn't mean that he or she needs to act authoritarian or be oppressive. Paul affirms the same in 2 Corinthians 1:24 as does Peter in 1 Peter 5:3. Pagan leaders in New Testament times were often ruthless, authoritarian figures who attempted to subject their people. Many men today have falsely interpreted their leadership as domination over women, and some treat their wives much as the pagan leaders subjugated their followers. For example, I am aware of some who will not allow their wives to spend any money, go anywhere by themselves, or spend time with their friends without their permission. They feel as if they must be in total control of their wives at all times. This is a dominant-passive relationship that some have espoused under the name of Christianity, when actually this is the kind of oppressive, authoritarian leadership that Christ condemns.

By contrast, in verses 26–28 Christ teaches that responsible servant leaders are to serve and sacrifice for their followers (Peter teaches the same in 1 Peter 5:2–3). Just as he came to earth not to be served, but to serve (v. 26), so men are to serve their wives. This means among other things that just as Christ always cared about and honored people throughout His ministry, so men serve their wives by caring for them and honoring them. This means that men can trust their wives with the finances, encourage them to develop healthy relations with other people, especially women, and encourage them to develop and use their God-given talents and abilities without feeling threatened. Men should value their wives as individuals and let them know that they are on their team and want to support them in what they do.

Also, as Christ sacrificed for many, so men are to make sacrifices for their wives and the women in their lives. Men must be willing to put aside their preoccupation with themselves, their interests, and their careers to address the needs and interests of their wives. This involves such matters as observing and listening to their wives. Men need to be aware of what their wives, fiancees, or girlfriends are experiencing in life and how they feel about those experiences. And men need to listen with insight and sensitivity to a woman's ideas. I will develop this sacrificial concept in greater detail in chapter 7, because in light of the Cross, it is an important element that the New Testament adds to the relationship of a man and a woman (Eph. 5:25).

Initiative

I believe that the man is responsible to take the initiate or move toward his wife, spiritually, emotionally, and physically. In Genesis 2:24, the man is to leave his father and mother. The implication is that he's to move toward his wife. This doesn't imply that wives aren't to show initiative in the relationship. An aspect of a man's leadership, however, is initiative or proactivity, as opposed to spiritual and emotional lethargy. It's the man's responsibility to assume the leadership of his family. He's to keep his finger on the spiritual and emotional pulse of his wife and family.

Currently, far too many (if not most) Christian men leave this up to their wives. They are too busy with other so-called more important things, usually work-related. But what could be more important than the spiritual and emotional health of their families? A man must ask himself, At death what kind of legacy will I leave for my family? Will my wife and kids remember me best for my work or the relationships that I have cultivated with them? We will see later in Genesis 3 that the underlying issue in a man's failure to lead is his feelings of incompetence, which are a result of the Fall. In becoming preoccupied with other things, many men have abandoned their responsibility for spiritual leadership.

Protection

There are also times when men as leaders need to be protective of their wives. When we study Genesis 3, we'll discover that Adam failed Eve when Satan tempted her. One way he failed her was not being protective of her. We will examine this in more detail in the next chapter, where I believe we'll see that Adam was present during Eve's temptation and could have intervened but didn't, and thus failed her as a man.

There are times when men as leaders need to be protective of their wives. Adam wasn't protective of Eve and failed her as a man.

Men today can recoup, essentially recover their manhood and be more protective of women. We can be there for them spiritually. We can learn much from Satan's temptation of Eve. As men, we can become spiritual leaders and intervene when we see the evil one subtly tempting our wives in to disobey in some way or fall away from God. We can be there for them in other ways. One is the prevention of emotional abuse. Not only do some men abuse their own wives, but they will abuse other men's wives if allowed to do so. You can detect an abuser by his attitude toward women and how he treats them within the church as well as in the marketplace. Abusers do not properly value women and will speak down to them or give them a difficult time. That's when a man needs to intervene and politely but firmly correct the situation.

Provision

There is some evidence in Genesis that a man carries the primary responsibility to provide for his wife and family. In Genesis 2, God placed man in a perfect environment with a perfect employment. An aspect of his employment was to work and take care of the environment (Paradise). God had placed certain trees in Paradise to supply him with food. It would appear that Adam took care of these trees and ate from them. It was in this way that he initially provided for himself and his family (Eve).

This doesn't mean, however, that a woman can't assist a man in that provision. God created the woman to help Adam (Gen. 2:18). It makes sense, therefore, that she would help him take care of Paradise. Today, this help could naturally extend to her pursuit of a personal career outside the home as well as working in the home. The Proverbs 31 woman appears to assist her husband through various business ventures (vv. 16, 24). It would be a mistake, however, for a woman or a man to pursue a career at the expense of the family. The woman in Proverbs 31 seems to put her family first (vv. 15, 21, 27). A primary application today of putting family first is the care of children. While children are young (preschoolers), they need the care and nurturing of a parent, not an institution such as day care or a relative.

Involvement

Men need to be intimately involved in the lives of their wives. I believe that this also is an aspect of a man's leaving his father and mother and moving toward his wife. Far too often men tend to isolate themselves emotionally and physically from their wives. The typical American male has imbibed deeply from the image of the 1940s and 1950s view of masculinity. He pictures himself as a man, which often means "don't let 'em see you cry." Our culture in the first half of the twentieth century sent a clear message to men that they must be tough which, being interpreted, means unemotional. To show too much emotion, especially tears, is a sign of weakness—that you're not in control (Gen. 43:30–31, 45:1–2). Our fathers bought into this concept and modeled it for us. In addition, what many of us don't realize is that men are afraid of their emotions. Just under the surface, we're afraid that our feelings will betray us and demonstrate to others what we quietly suspect—that we are incompetent as men.

While the second half of the twentieth century has seriously called much of this macho thinking into question, this view has still exercised a deep influence on far too many men. The result is that if men are to convince themselves that they are real men, they must come across as rugged, unemotional individualists. They don't need anyone's help; they can do it on their own. Thus they isolate themselves from their wives and their own emotions as they crawl into their own little cocoons of illegitimate manhood.

Strength

There are also times when men need to be strong with their wives. In Genesis 3, we will discover that as the result of the Fall, women will experience a natural predisposition to challenge a man's leadership. We'll see that this also took place later in the lives of others in Genesis, such as Abraham and Sarah (Gen. 16), and Rachel and Jacob (Gen. 30). Even though God promised infertile Sarah and Rachel each a child, they grew impatient and attempted to take matters into their own hands. They took control, offering to their husbands other women through whom they would produce offspring. The result was disaster—you can read about it in Genesis 16 and 30.

There are times when men need to be spiritually strong for their wives. To be weak is to back away from your manhood.

My point is that in both these situations, the men, Abraham and Isaac, weren't strong. And they failed their wives as well. They should have shown some strength and exercised a little leadership. Instead, they backed away from their responsibilities as Adam had with Eve, and thus in a sense backed away from their manhood. These men could have encouraged their wives by loving and caring for them even though things had not gone as these women had hoped.

Today, every woman will experience difficult times in her life, and she'll be tempted to move without waiting for God. And it's during those times that they need their men to be strong for them and to encourage them to wait on God's promises. In short, they need for their men to be men.

Decisiveness

A close companion of a man's strength is decisiveness. This is not to say that the man makes all the decisions in the relationship. It's to say that as the leader, he's responsible for those decisions. The "buck" stops with him. There will be areas where he'll look to his wife for help. One area mentioned in Scripture is the management of the home (1 Tim. 5:14).

An aspect of strength in leadership is not shrinking back from decisions, but facing those decisions and not leaving them in the lap of your wife.

An aspect of strength in proactive leadership is not shrinking back from even the hard decisions. A man should face those decisions and not leave them in the lap of his wife. As the president of a corporation wouldn't attempt to make all the decisions by him- or herself, so the head of the family needs help from his wife. The president does, however, ultimately have to make those decisions, and he is responsible for them. Men tend to be good at this in the business world (their area of perceived competence) but not on the homefront (an area of perceived incompetence).

GOD DESIGNED EVE TO BE THE PRIMARY HELPER IN THEIR RELATIONSHIP

In Genesis 2:18, God designates Eve as Adam's suitable helper: "Then the Lord said, 'It is not good for the man to be alone. I will make a helper suitable for him.'" The term "suitable" means that she, not the animals, was suitable for a relationship with Adam. She was his equivalent; she shared his nature. She was like him, not the animals. I believe that God designated her to function as a helper because He designed her to be a suitable helper. Before the Fall, it was natural for her to want and to be a supportive helper in the garden. Again, God wouldn't ask her to do that which she was incapable of doing.

The problem with this responsibility for the contemporary woman concerns her personal worth. Doesn't being a helper imply functional inferiority, and doesn't that imply less worth as a person? The answer to both questions is no. The term "helper" is in no way demeaning to her as a woman because the same term is used of God in the Old Testament (Exod. 18:4; Deut. 33:7; 1 Sam. 7:12, and so on). Although God helps people, He's not inferior to any person. Old Testament scholar Allen Ross states: "The word essentially describes one who provides what is lacking in the man, who can do what the man alone cannot do. . . . The man was created in such a way that he needs the help of a partner."[5] Neither Eve nor anyone in that culture would have understood the concept as describing someone inferior.

But what then was Eve's role as a helper? How did she function to help Adam? She helped him fulfill God's image. Again, she provided that which was lacking in Adam—she completed him. Initially this involved reflecting or mirroring God's image (Gen. 1): co-ruling creation, reproducing life, relating to God and one another, and so on. Numerous, helpful modern illustrations come to mind. One compares him to the president of a corporation and her to the vice-president, not simply another employee. Those in the corporate world are well aware of the value of a good vice-president. Another illustration compares him to the point person on a team and her to the support person. The point person is clearly the leader but would not go far without the support person to supply that which the former lacks. Still another sees him as the coach of a team and her as the assistant coach rather than just a player.

While helpful, all these illustrations have a major flaw. The president, point person, and coach have more worth in the real world than the vice-president, support person, and assistant coach. Whether they should or shouldn't is another issue. (I believe that all are essentially equal in value while functionally different.) The important point is that most of us believe this to be true. That is why we pay the former more than the latter. Because they carry greater responsibility, we perceive them to have greater worth.

God designed and designated Eve to be Adam's helper—she helped him to fulfill God's image— she completed him.

Consequently, a better illustration is the relationship of the three members of the Trinity—specifically God the Father and God the

Son. In 1 Corinthians 11:3, Paul writes: "Now I want you to realize that the head of every man is Christ, and the head of the woman is man, and the head of Christ is God." The last part of this verse clearly teaches that God the Father is head of God the Son, Jesus Christ. (Paul also teaches this in 1 Cor. 3:23 and 1 Cor. 15:28.) But how could this be? The answer is that while the Son is equal to the Father, he also willingly submits himself to the leadership of the Father to accomplish their common purpose. In the same way, the woman, who is essentially equal to the man, willingly submits herself to his leadership to accomplish the purpose of God. In a very real sense, the woman as a supportive helper is serving her God much as the Savior served Him. She serves much like Christ when she helps her husband.

Eve's primary role was that of helper. She helped him in numerous ways. As with Adam, I've placed a few of them in a subset under helper (fig. 2). It includes such functions as following, responding, supporting, assisting, receiving, nurturing, and so on.

> ### THE WOMAN AS PRIMARY HELPER
> **She follows, responds, receives, supports, assists, nurtures, etc.**

(Figure 2)

Following

God has designated women such as Carol to function as supportive helpers. This does not mean that some women aren't excellent leaders as well as helpers, nor does it mean that there aren't situations in which women exercise leadership. There are times, however, when she follows her husband's leadership much as Christ follows the Father's leadership. She is much more than a follower, but she is also a follower. As the president of a large corporation consults with his or her vice-presidents before making a major decision to gain their wisdom and advice on a business-related topic, so a husband seeks input from his wife. She's a major player in the relationship. But after the decision is made, the vice-presidents follow that decision. If she doesn't follow her husband's leadership, then she calls his leadership into question and places the relationship in jeopardy.

The problem in some relationships, however, is that the man won't lead or he leads poorly. Also, some men lead well in the work environment where they feel competent but not in the home environment where they feel less competent. This, too, puts the marriage in jeopardy. After the couple marries, there is little a woman can do about the dysfunctional relationship other than to encourage his leadership and to pray for him. Her temptation will be to force him to lead. But this never works. She can't change him. The only person who can change him is either himself or God. The place to catch this is before marriage. The tip to discovering his leadership ability for the future is examining his leadership ability in the present. The future bride must ask herself, Has he been a leader in our relationship so far? And equally important, Am I willing to follow his leadership?

But isn't being a follower an admission of inferiority? It's no less demeaning for a woman to follow the lead of her husband than it is for Christ the Son to follow the lead of God the Father. First Corinthians 11:4–5, 7 teaches that in following her husband's leadership, a wife honors and values her husband much as the man honors God when he follows Him.

Responding

Genesis 2:24 speaks of a man leaving his father and mother and being united to his wife. A part of what's taking place is that he is moving away from them toward her. That relationship with his parents will not be what it used to be. He will subordinate it to his new relationship with his wife. Whereas a man's father was the leader, now the man himself has become the leader of his own family. Moving toward his wife is an aspect of a husband's proactivity in leadership. As a new leader and his wife's leader, he's moving toward her physically and emotionally. Therefore, one way she completes him is to respond to his initiative—to be there for him emotionally and physically. While she must have someone to respond to, he must have someone to initiate with.

This is a major problem in many marriages today. The man may have never emotionally moved away from his parents. A man's father could still be the controlling person in his life and now in his marriage. More than likely, however, his mother is that controlling influence. Regardless, the husband has not initiated well with his wife throughout their marriage so that she has not been able to respond well to him either emotionally or physically. He may have abused or abandoned her and thus abused her dignity as a responder. In doing this, he has to some degree undermined her womanhood. Consequently, she finds it difficult to respond to him and be the woman God has designed her to be.

Receiving

A woman completes her husband by receiving him physically as well as emotionally and spiritually. An aspect of her responding to him is her receiving him sexually. In the marriage act, he enters, she receives. So far I have discussed the marriage partnership primarily from a spiritual and emotional perspective. An important part of that relationship and their completing one another, however, is how they relate physically. If it wasn't important, then Paul wouldn't have taken so much time to address it in 1 Corinthians 7:1–7, nor Solomon in Song of Songs. The physical relationship too is reflective of a couples creative design and intent. Essentially, God designed and formed him to penetrate, her to receive.

When a husband exercises loving, responsible leadership with his wife, she finds it much easier to respond to him and receive him physically.

This involves her acceptance of him. When she's receptive and warm to him sexually, it's usually reflective of their relationship as a whole. Their relationship and her acceptance of him sexually serves as litmus test of how well he's doing emotionally and spiritually. When he exercises intimate, responsible leadership in serving his wife, she finds it much easier to respond to him and receive him physically.

Most bookstores keep a large supply of books on hand that deal with physical sex. This topic has always been popular because the public in general and men in particular are concerned, perhaps obsessed at times, with what many refer to today as "good sex." Outside of marriage and Christianity, this preoccupation results in significant tragedy and harsh abuse. Within marriage, however, what men, especially Christian men, need to learn is that the best sex (sexual intercourse) is preceded by emotional and spiritual intercourse. When a man exercises intimate, Christlike leadership with his wife (in a very real sense spiritual and emotional intercourse), she is much more receptive to him sexually as her lover. Men mistakenly tend to equate intimacy and romance with sex. This has much to do with the intensity of that part of the male sexual drive that most women don't understand. While women understand the connection between intimacy and sex, they don't equate the two. While she is to receive him sexually (1 Cor. 7:5), he would be wise to initiate with her emotionally and spiritually as well as sexually. This should take place daily and not just prior to physical sex.

It's so much easier for a wife to accept her husband and be receptive to him physically when he understands these matters. While Scripture doesn't dwell on this topic, it doesn't ignore it either. A man can learn much about his responsibilities to his wife, and she can learn much about her receptivity of him in Song of Songs, or Song of Solomon, in the Old Testament as well as in 1 Corinthians 7:1–8 in the New Testament.

Supporting

It's important to men that they feel that their wives are supportive of their leadership. He needs to feel that she's on his team, that she's pulling for him in spite of his inadequacies. Much of his relationship with her focuses on their home-world as opposed to their work-world. While men tend to feel at least adequate in their jobs and even look to them for their strokes, they don't feel as good about the job they are doing in leading their wives and families. The marrige relationship is a mystery for so many men.

It's important to men that they feel that their wives are supportive of their leadership.

Consequently, if a wife doesn't show support, or if a husband thinks his wife is not supportive of him, then he feels undermined as a man. For example, a father may discipline a child in a certain manner. The mother may disagree with his method but make the mistake of challenging him in front of the child. She has just emotionally emasculated him and undermined his leadership in the eyes of their child. While he may have been wrong, she should have handled it more discreetly—she could have discussed the matter with him in private. Her former behavior is relationally destructive and dishonors him, while the latter is relationally supportive and honors him. By rationally discussing the matter in private, he feels less threatened and is more willing to admit and correct his mistakes.

When a man senses that his wife doesn't support him, he often retaliates by demanding her support or emotionally abandoning their relationship and his responsibility to lead. Deep inside, he suspects that her nonsupport is reflective of his leadership abilities, and that he's not getting the job done, or he's not doing it well. While this may be true, it's very hard on the male ego. Rather than trying to improve, he tends to move away from his failure and focus his efforts on what he believes are his areas of strength.

Assisting

A woman helps a man by assisting him. There are so many things a woman can do that a man can't. That she's an assisting helper serves not to demean her but to enhance her womanhood. She is as talented and gifted as he is, if not more so. In a very real sense she supplies what he's lacking. When she marries him, she brings her many talents and abilities together with his, and thus together they can accomplish so much more for the Savior as a complementary team than individually.

There are so many things a woman can do that a man can't. That she's a talented assisting helper serves not to demean her but to enhance her womanhood.

It's very important that men recognize that every woman is a "ten" in some area. God has gifted her to serve well in many significant areas. And men should recognize and encourage women to grow and develop in those areas. This has been difficult for some men, especially since women began to move into vocational areas once reserved for men only. This is true of the blue-collar work world as well as the white-collar world. Women are becoming skilled plumbers and electricians who work with their hands, as well as corporate executives who work in the marketplace. I believe that in the family context, weak men are threatened by their wive's talents, whereas strong men feel assisted and thus complemented.

The ministry of Howard and Jeanne Hendricks is an excellent example of a couple where the wife assists and completes her husband well. Dr. Hendricks has taught at Dallas Theological Seminary for over thirty years and is known worldwide for his expertise as an insightful Bible teacher and expert on the family. When I first sat under his ministry as a seminarian in the 1970s, I was well aware of Professor Hendricks and his ministry. One of the reasons that I attended Dallas Seminary was learn from him and his teaching. I was also aware of Jeanne Hendricks because of her involvement with women students and students' wives. As they've experienced the empty-nest syndrome, however, Jeanne now often travels with and ministers alongside Dr. Hendricks. Whereas he authored many of his earlier books, now they are coauthored with Jeanne. The reason is obvious. By assisting him, she brings a dimension to their ministry that he can't supply, and vice versa. Together they have had a far more effective ministry than he by himself.

The leader-helper roles are at the very foundation of authentic womanhood and manhood. They help a woman to understand what it means to be a woman and a man, a man.

I can't stress enough the importance of understanding the leader-helper function of Adam and Eve in Genesis 2. It's the key to understanding today how men and women are to relate to one another, especially in the 1990s and into the early twenty-first century when the ideas of roles and distinctions between men and women will become so blurred. It's true that feminism has helped women in many ways. But the feminist attempt to eradicate male-female distinctions has confused more than it's helped. The leader-helper roles are at the very foundation of authentic womanhood and manhood. They help a woman to understand what it means to be a woman and a man, a man. Also, this complementary partnership is foundational to understanding Genesis 3 and what the rest of the Bible teaches about

womanhood and manhood. You can't understand Genesis 3 and the
Fall without understanding how male and female complement each
other.

A couple of crucial question. Isn't the leader-helper function
teaching male dominance, which is another word for abuse? Isn't this
encouraging a dominant-passive relationship where the woman is little
more than a doormat? The answer is that physical and emotional
dominance (abuse) is the result of the Fall (Gen. 3:16), not the concept
of godly headship. I'll say more about this important concept in
chapter 5. We get a feel for what it was like to live in a helper-leader
relationship from the subsets above. Genesis 2:25, however, provides
us with a clear snapshot of Adam's and Eve's complementary
partnership in Paradise: "The man and his wife were both naked, and
they felt no shame." Their outward, physical nakedness pictured an
inward, emotional-spiritual nakedness. They were completely open
and transparent with each other. There wasn't any fear of vulnerability
or exploitation. Adam and Eve experienced a rich intimacy. I suspect
that they talked about things that really mattered without
embarrassment or threat of repercussion. They totally accepted and
honored one another and the other's interests. I would imagine that
when she spoke, he carefully listened with insight and sensitivity to
her ideas, and he heard not only her words but the feelings that
embraced those words.

The text also says that "they felt no shame." Shame is a by-product
of sin (Gen. 3:7). One component of sin involves the wrongful
exploitation of one's vulnerability that causes one pain. It results in a
deep sense of exposure or emotional nakedness. One's intimacy has
been compromised in the worst way. People who experience shame
see themselves as flawed and of questionable worth. Those who
undergo extreme shame see themselves as so flawed as to be of no
worth. They ask, Why would anyone love me? I'm not worthy of
anyone's love. Adam and Eve knew none of this in Genesis 1–2. I
suspect that they shared a strong sense of worth and personal
significance. They valued one another and believed that together they
were accomplishing something significant for God.

One arrives at the end of this chapter and Genesis 2 and asks, What
happened? The relationship between men and women today isn't the
complementary partnership described in Genesis 2:25. It's not even
close. And most couples like Randy and Carol go into a relationship

with expectations of one another comparable to verse 25. But even before the honeymoon is over, reality quickly sets in. What goes wrong? The answer is found in Genesis 3.

DISCUSSION QUESTIONS

For Singles

If you're a single man, and you're in a serious relationship with a woman that may lead to marriage, think through the following questions:

1. Can I function as a man with this woman? Can I lead her? Can I initiate with her? Can I protect her and at proper times show strength with her? Do I understand intimacy, and am I willing to get involved in her life at an intimate level? What makes you think so? What evidence is there in the relationship so far that indicates you will do any of these things?

2. Will I function as a man with this woman? Will I attempt to lead her? Will I initiate, protect, honor, and be strong with her while not dominating her? In short, am I really interested in being a man with her?

3. Is she a Christian? If not, why not? Are you a Christian? If not, why not? Should a Christian marry a non-Christian? (Read 2 Cor. 6:14.) How can you be the spiritual leader if one or both of you isn't a Christian? What does this tell you about the future of your relationship? Does this knowledge make a difference?

4. Assuming that both of you are Christians, will you be the spiritual leader in this relationship? Who is stronger spiritually, you or her? How do you know this? Why is one stronger than the other? If she is stronger, can you lead her? What can you do about this spiritual inequity?

5. Will she let you lead her? How do you know? What evidence is there in the relationship so far that indicates that she will follow your leadership? If there is no evidence, what should you do? Have you talked about your relationship?

If you're a single woman and in a serious relationship with a man that could lead to marriage, think through the following questions:

1. Can I function as a woman with this man? Do I feel free to be his helper? Can I follow his leadership, or do I find myself often leading in our relationship? Can I support, respond to, and assist him? Do I trust him? What evidence is there in your relationship so far that indicates you can be his supportive helper?

2. Even if most of your answers to these questions are no, do you plan to marry him anyway? Why? Does this make sense?

3. Will you function as a woman with this man? Will you be his helper? Will you follow his leadership? If not, why not? Will you support and assist him? Have you supported and assisted him thus far in your relationship?

4. Is he a Christian? How do you know for sure? Are you a Christian? How do you know for sure? If either one of you isn't a Christian, should you get married? (Read 2 Cor. 6:14.) How can you possibly help him if either of you isn't a Christian?

5. Assuming that both of you are Christians, will he be the spiritual leader in your family? Why or why not? Is he the spiritual leader at present? Why or why not? If the answer is no, do you think that things will be any different after you're married? Do you believe that you'll be able to change him after you're married? You must realize that you can't change him! The only one who can change him is himself or God. What makes you think he's going to change? Are you being realistic?

6. Does he ever dominate or abuse you emotionally or physically? If the answer is yes, what are you doing about it? Have you talked about it? Have you talked with a professional about the problem (a counselor, minister, priest, psychologist, psychiatrist)? Are you viewing this relationship realistically? Should you marry an abuser, knowing that you can't change him?

For Marrieds

If you're a married man, think through the following questions.

1. Are you functioning as a man with your wife? That is, are you the leader in your family? Do you ever initiate in any way with your wife? Are you involved emotionally and spiritually in her life, or is she on her own? Do your really listen to her? Do you protect her and at the proper time show a healthy strength with her?

2. Are you a Christian? Why or why not? Is your wife a Christian? Why or why not? How do you know? How has the question of Christianity affected your marriage? What do you plan to do about it?

3. Are you the spiritual leader in your relationship or do you leave that to your wife? Why or why not? What would your wife say if she were asked this question? If the answer is no, why aren't you the spiritual leader? Who is stronger spiritually, you or your wife? Why? If she is stronger than you, what can/will you do about it?

4. Were you ever abused in any way as a child or adolescent? If yes, what were the circumstances? Do you ever abuse your wife physically or emotionally? If yes, how and why? Have you talked about this problem? What are you doing about it? Have you talked with, or are you getting help from, a professional (a minister, priest, counselor, psychologist, or psychiatrist)? If not, why not? Is there any reason to believe that without help you'll change?

If you're a married woman, think through the following questions:

1. Are you functioning as a woman with your husband? That is, are you a supportive helper? Why or why not? Do you make an effort to respond to him, to follow his leadership, and to support him in what he does? Why or why not?

2. Are you willing to be his supportive helper? Why or why not? Are you willing to respond to him, to follow his leadership, and to support him in what he does? Why or why not?

3. Are you a Christian? Why or why not? Is your husband a Christian? Why or why not? Are you both Christians or is one of you a non-Christian? How has this affected your relationship? Is it a partnership?

4. Has anyone ever abused you as a child or adolescent? If yes, who and how? How has it affected your marriage? Does your husband know about it? If not, why haven't you told him? Have you sought help from a professional such as a counselor, minister, psychologist, or psychiatrist?

5. Is your husband ever abusive in any way? If yes, how and why? Was he abusive before marriage? What have you done about his abuse? Why do you allow him to abuse you? Have you talked about it? If not, why not? What do you plan to do about it? Is there any reason to believe that things will change if you don't deal with the problem?

Notes

1. John H. Sailhammer, *The Pentateuch as Narrative* (Grand Rapids: Zondervan Publishing House, 1992), p. 101.

2. Steve Kinny, "He never asked her for a date because she always had one," *The Dallas Morning News*, April 9, 1995, p. 10F.

3. Sharon Begley, "Gray Matters," *Newsweek*, March 27, 1995, pp. 48–54.

4. Raymond C. Ortlund, "Male-Female Equality and Male Headship" *in Recovering Biblical Manhood & Womanhood*, ed. John Piper and Wayne Grudem (Wheaton, Ill.: Crossway Books, 1991), p. 481, fn. 25.

5. Allen P. Ross, *Creation & Blessing: A Guide to the Study and Exposition of Genesis* (Grand Rapids: Baker Book House, 1988), p. 126.

PART II

The Corruption
of Human Sexuality

Today's boomers and Xers such as Randy and Carol are quick to point out that Genesis 1 and 2 are not the real world as they know it. Men and women simply don't relate that way. Genesis 3 is the real world; it is what most couples experience in their relationships as men and women. What happened? The answer is found in Genesis 3. This key, pivotal chapter has everything to do with their sexuality—Adam as a man, and Eve as a woman. In chapter 3, Satan tempts Adam and Eve through their sexuality to disobey their Creator with disastrous consequences.

3

The Temptation of Sexuality

Where Were You, Adam?

The Boeing 747 accelerated down the runway, then climbed quickly but gracefully into the clear, blue sky over the Dallas-Fort Worth Airport. The initial thrust politely pinned Carol and Randy back in their seats and then gently released them. They were on their way to the beautiful sun-drenched beaches of Honolulu, Hawaii, to celebrate their second wedding anniversary. Both were excited about this opportunity to get away from it all. The past two years were filled with long, stressful hours at work, leadership of the Newly Marrieds Class at church, and the numerous adjustments newlyweds make when first living with one another.

It hadn't been an easy two years despite the excellent premarital counseling provided by the Christian counselor at Fellowship Community Church. Like so many other couples, Randy and Carol had innocently assumed otherwise. And at times both were a little surprised as each partner failed to live up to the other's expectations. Their counselor had warned them that even early in their marriage there would be disappointments, but somehow the message failed to penetrate the romantic fog that had moved in and settled over their engagement.

Randy understood clearly from the Scriptures that he was to be the responsible servant-leader in their relationship, and Carol understood her function as the supportive helper. Nevertheless, when Randy, as a new husband, took some responsibility for their relationship, the marriage game turned more complex than he had imagined. For example, Randy believed that they needed more counseling, but Carol did not respond favorably. She refused! She believed that they could work through their problems on their own and refused outside help.

Both believed they had worked through the clouds of dysfunction that had cast such an ominous shadow over the early, difficult years of growing up in their families in Dallas. Their past, however, was still very much a part of the present and would become a vital part of their future as well.

As the flight attendant announced that the captain was about to turn off the Fasten Your Seat Belts sign, Randy's thoughts turned to the joys of relaxing with Carol on the beach as they soaked up a few rays together. His primary complaint thus far with their relationship was that Carol was too controlling. Every time he stood up to bat and exercised some responsibility as a husband, Carol threw him pitches that were impossible to hit. He always struck out even though he rarely took a swing.

For example, they both owned separate cars. However, Carol was used to buying a new car every other year. Her dad always came up with a sizable down payment that made a new vehicle affordable. The first time this came up in the marriage, Randy said no. He was convinced that they could not afford it, and he wanted them to provide for themselves. Despite his objections, Carol bought the car. One day he came home from work, and it was sitting in their driveway. He bristled on the inside but chose to say nothing about either the incident or his anger at what she had done.

As the attendant smiled and gently pressed an oxygen mask up to her face to demonstrate how they should respond in case of an emergency, Carol's thoughts turned to their trip, its purpose, and their young, two-year marriage. She had been disappointed with Randy's passivity in the relationship. She couldn't understand why he seemed so reluctant to lead and show more initiative, yet when he did, she found herself quietly resisting him. His response was to back off and let her have her own way, which made her feel good but set off an alarm somewhere in the deep recesses of her mind. For example, Carol's dad thought it would be nice if they bought a house. He offered to help the couple with a sizable down payment. Randy was not comfortable with this offer. When he and Carol discussed it, he gave her two reasons. First, right or wrong, he did not believe that they could afford the mortgage payments. Second, he felt that this was her dad's way of appeasing his conscience over not spending more time with Carol. Rather than visit her and use it as an opportunity to talk with her about the things in their lives that really mattered, he would buy her gifts. He saw what this was doing to Carol, and he was attempting to protect her.

However, Carol did not see it this way. He was responsible to make the final decision, but that did not mean that she had to like it. She scolded Randy and said that he was too tight. For several days she said little to him. When he asked her what was wrong, she said, "Nothing." He would push no further. During that time they were visiting another couple who asked about the house. The husband argued that Randy was wrong, and Carol was quick to agree with him, siding against Randy. Randy believed that this was personal—not something to be aired in public. He felt undermined, even betrayed. Carol could tell that he was visibly upset, but he chose to internalize the whole affair. He said nothing, fearing her response.

As the bright morning sun glinted off the plane's wing, Carol wished so much that on occasion Randy would stand up to her and be strong, that he would not let her have her own way so often. In short, she wished that he would be a man.

Carol's and Randy's difficulties in marriage, however, are not new to the twenty-first century. Actually, they can be easily traced back to the very beginning. Their marriage experience essentially pictures that of Adam and Eve in Genesis 3:1–5. Randy and Carol's first two years of marriage closely parallel the early relationship of the first couple. Genesis 3 is a pivotal chapter that has everything to do with Adam's and Eve's sexuality and what it means to be an authentic man and woman. And verses 1–5 provide a classic picture of evil solicitation as Satan tempts the first couple in terms of their sexuality to disobey God. The account naturally breaks into two movements. In the first, the evil one entices Eve as a woman to doubt and disobey God. In the second, he tempts Adam as a man to follow in her footsteps.

SATAN TEMPTS EVE
AS A WOMAN TO DISOBEY GOD

Satan's Strategy

In Genesis 3:1 one of the animals under their dominion, the serpent, approaches Eve and initiates a disclaimer on what he believes is one of the major disadvantages of living in Paradise—obedience to God. Though the text doesn't give the serpent's identity, Revelation 12:9 and 20:2 purposely identify him as the devil, or Satan. As a high-ranking angel (Ezek. 28:12), he had attempted a cosmic rebellion before Genesis 1. He led a coup in heaven against God only to be cast out from His presence (Ezek. 28:16–19). Now he appears again in Genesis 3 to attempt another coup on earth. Why not try a second time? After all, he has nothing to lose; God has already determined his destiny (Matt. 25:41).

Genesis 3:1 describes him as "more crafty," or more subtle, than any of the animals. Adam and Eve are dealing with an extremely intelligent spirit being—you or I would be no match for him, and neither were they, as they were about to find out. The Old Testament was written in the Hebrew language, and in verse 1 there's a Hebrew wordplay that connects the term "naked" describing Adam and Eve in 2:25 with crafty or subtle, describing the serpent in 3:1. The point is, in his subtlety, he will take advantage of Adam an Eve's sexuality; the temptation relates directly to their sexual identity. Genesis 1 and 2 has much to say about God's plan for Adam's and Eve's sexuality, and it's only natural that Satan would attack them at this point. According to 2 Corinthians 2:11, he devises various schemes that he might outwit us. Here his scheme is a twofold strategy of temptation that assaults Eve's womanhood and attacks God's character. Let's eavesdrop.

He Approaches Eve, Not Adam. After introducing the serpent, Genesis 3:1 reveals the initial victim and target of his deception: "He said to the woman." God is the initiator in Genesis 1 and 2; Satan becomes the initiator in Genesis 3. This satanic deception begins with "the woman" (later to be named Eve), not Adam. In short, he by-passes Adam as the responsible party and targets Eve, Adam's vulnerable helper. He cleverly, subtly takes advantage of her vulnerability (Gen. 2:25) to corrupt her sexuality—what it means to be a woman.

Satan cleverly takes advantage of Eve's vulnerability to corrupt her sexuality—what it means to be a woman.

Temptation is a spiritual matter, and Adam is spiritually responsible for their relationship. Satan knows that and subtly chooses to sidestep Adam to attack Eve. While it's doubtful from the rest of the story that Adam would have fared any better than Eve, it appears that Satan, as an initiator, avoids Adam, who as the leader is also an initiator, and attacks

Eve—a primary responder. As we watch the diabolical scheme unfold, our response is to shake our heads and mutter a reluctant, "How clever."

He Assaults God's Character. To better understand this narrative, I have placed myself in Eve's position. The Tempter disguises himself as an inquisitive serpent, a subordinate creature, and approaches her with what on the surface appears to be a rather harmless question: "Did God really say, 'You must not eat from any tree in the garden'?" How innocent. What could possibly be wrong with that? She goes on to explain, somewhat inaccurately, in verses 2–3 that the serpent is mistaken. God has given them free access to the fruit of any of the trees in the garden except the tree of the knowledge of good and evil.

The conversation now takes a sudden, unexpected turn when the so-called harmless creature in verse 4 flatly denies God's word with the emphatic contradiction, "You will not surely die." This is where she should have caught on to what was taking place. It's understandable how her guard might not have been up before, but it should be now. In essence, the Tempter calls God a liar. In Genesis 2:17, God emphatically told Adam that he was not to eat from the tree of the knowledge of good and evil or "you will surely die." Satan's goal is to inject a degree of doubt in her mind regarding God's very character. He's boldly saying that God can't be trusted.

In verse 5, Satan explains that God is selfishly holding something back: "For God knows that when you eat of it your eyes will be opened, and you will be like God, knowing good and evil." The implication is obvious—she can be her own God. The appeal is irresistible. All of us would prefer to be like God—to be in control of our lives—to be our own god. Not to be in control, to let another control you, is to be out of control and most vulnerable. This is frightening. God made you from Adam, Eve, and you are frail humanity. Now here's your chance! Knowledge is power, and God is holding back the knowledge and wisdom that will give you ultimate power over your life. At last you can be in absolute control. Eat and enjoy your power.

Eve's Response

Eve Becomes the Spokesperson. Eve's response to the Tempter is twofold. In verses 1–5, she does all the talking! Except possibility to clear his throat on occasion, Adam doesn't say a word until verse 10.

Eve spoke when she should have been silent. When Satan clearly contradicted God's command, "You will not surely die," she should have ended the conversation (Paul implies this in 1 Timothy 2:11–14). It was time to turn the situation over to Adam. Instead, she reverses their proper roles and leads when she should have followed.

Eve Sins. Second, in verse 6, she takes the bait—she believes and eats. Essentially, she shifts her trust from God to Satan. She shifts her devotion from her Creator, who has proved to be compassionate, gracious, faithful, and loving (Exod. 34:6–7) to a subordinate creature. In verse 6 she reasons: It looks good, it tastes good, it will make me wise, why not? However, it doesn't stop there. As the new leader in their relationship, she initiates and gives some to Adam in verse 6, and he eats as well.

SATAN TEMPTS ADAM
AS A MAN TO DISOBEY GOD

Satan's scheme is to use Eve to by-pass Adam, the responsible leader, and it works. In the temptation process, Satan manages to entice and corrupt Adam as well as Eve. As a man, Adam fails Eve, God, and himself in two vital ways.

Adam Fails to Initiate and Lead

Where was Adam, the responsible head, while Satan tempted Eve? Verse 6 seems to indicate that he was present during much of, if not the entire, deception: "She also gave to her husband, *who was with her*, and he ate it" (italics mine). Also, the verbs are all plural and that would seem to include Adam. Adam is tragically quiet throughout the temptation process—he says nothing until verse 10. This was his failure. As the temptation progressed, he was irresponsibly quiet. His silence was deafening. Whereas Eve was talking when she should have been listening, Adam was quiet when he should have been leading.

The temptation presents the first real test of his manhood as a spiritual leader in his relationship with the woman. Tragically, he failed that test. Later, in Genesis 3:17, God says: "Because you listened to your wife, and ate from the tree about which I commanded you, 'You must not eat of it.'. . ." Adam functioned as a responder rather than a leader and an initiator. Verse 17 is saying that he listened when he should have led. Not that it's wrong for a man to listen to his wife, but not when she entices him to sin.

This raises the obvious question, What went wrong with Adam? Why did he eat, and why didn't he show some initiative and lead? He could have served and protected Eve by intervening in the temptation. First Timothy 2:14 adds to his dilemma by pointing out that he knew what he was doing when he took the fruit from Eve's extended hand and ate, whereas she was deceived. Paul writes: "And Adam was not the one deceived; it was the woman who was deceived and became a sinner."

> *Whereas Eve was talking when she should have been quiet, Adam was quiet when he should have been leading.*

Some, most likely men, might imply that his behavior was a last-minute expression of his love for Eve or an act of loyalty toward her, that he was trying desperately to recoup and come to her aid. There is no evidence in the passage, however, to suggest this. More likely, being present during the temptation, he listened to Satan and took the bait as well. Eve's temptation was Adam's temptation. Adam had it all. God had blessed him by placing him in a perfect environment with a perfect employment, but it wasn't enough. Adam wanted more. Like Eve, the thought of being his own god was too much and so he ate. Little did he realize that he was being used, that he was a vital part in Satan's coup—a mere pawn on the proverbial chessboard in what had become a vast cosmic conflict.

Adam Abandons Eve

The tragedy of Genesis 3:1–5 is multiple. Adam has given in to Satan's seduction, Satan has used and abused him, and he hardly knows it yet. Adam has abandoned his Creator who has unconditionally loved and blessed him and will in time forgive him. In the midst of all this, Adam has failed Eve in the worst way. During her time of need, rather than serve her, he abandoned her. Though he was physically present, he was not there for her spiritually nor emotionally. God had designed him to complete her. That would have been leadership. Instead, he left her on her own. He deserted his role as a responsible leader and thus deserted her in the process. In essence, he failed her as a man—he abandoned his manhood.

This abandonment created a number of ripples that pass through their relationship and impact us today. One is Adam's failure as spiritual protector. As a leader, he was primarily responsible for the spiritual and emotional well-being of this family. Paul develops this concept in 1 Timothy 3. In verse 1, he encourages men to seek to become overseers—a position of spiritual responsibility and leadership in the church. Then in verse 4, he points out that as an overseer: "[a man] must manage his own family well and see that his children obey him with proper respect. (If anyone does not know how to manage his own family, how can he take care of God's church?),"

> *Adam failed Eve in the worst way. During her time of need, he abandoned her. While he was physically present, he wasn't there for her spiritually or emotionally.*

An aspect of a man managing his family well is protecting his wife in the arena of spiritual warfare. We shouldn't have to ask the question, Where was Adam when Eve needed him the most? The strong spiritual leader would have exercised his God-given dominion over creation and exercise dominion over the serpent as well. He would have stepped forward, interrupted the conversation, and rebuked the creature. The Savior has modeled this for men in the Gospels. Instructive is Christ's encounter with Peter in Matthew 16:22–23. When the Savior announced to the disciples that he would have to suffer and die, Peter took him aside and rebuked him (v. 22). Knowing that this was Satan-inspired, Christ turned to Peter and said: "Get behind me Satan! You are a stumbling block to me; you do not have in mind the things of God, but the things of men" (v. 23).

Another aspect of spiritual leadership, and a second ripple, is the need for men to be strong concerning their wives. Showing strength does not mean dominating or abusing a woman in any way. A man is never to slap his wife around either physically, emotionally, or spiritually. Most men understand physical abuse. Few realize that often in a relationship with a woman they can emotionally abuse her. Fewer yet understand spiritual abuse. An example of spiritual abuse is when Christian men dominate their wives and call it headship. This domination involves treating women as inferior persons. It fails essentially to recognize them as co-equal image-bearers. We'll explore this further in verse 16 (chapt. 5).

Showing strength in Genesis 3:1–5 means that when Adam saw where the conversation was going, he should have taken charge of the situation. He should have asserted himself as the spiritual leader. This goes hand in hand with protection. Eve may have objected to any interference—the desire to be in control of one's life, to be one's own God, is irresistible. But he would have needed to assert himself—to be proactive with her. He would have completed her by taking the lead and insisting that she follow his leadership and not Satan's.

WHO WAS TO BLAME?

How many times have you heard semi-biblically literate people, most often men, say: "If only Eve hadn't eaten that apple, we wouldn't be in the mess we're in today!" There are several problems with this statement. First, when the woman ate of the forbidden fruit, Adam had not yet named her Eve. In Genesis 2:23, he called her "woman," which in the twenty-first century seems a little derogatory. This is a Hebrew wordplay, however, connecting the terms "woman" and "man," which are very similar in the original language. The reason is that the term "woman," according to verse 23, means "taken out of man." It isn't until Genesis 3:20 that Adam calls her "Eve," which means "the mother of all the living."

Second, the Bible doesn't say anywhere that she ate an apple. According to Genesis 3:6, she ate fruit. It could have been an apple or an orange or some fruit native to the region. The important point is not what she ate, but that she ate. She sinned, not because of her taste buds, but because she disobeyed God's word. No one can disobey God without consequences.

Third, and most important, is that no one should place all the blame for the Fall on the woman. From Genesis 3, this should seem obvious, but it isn't the case. Throughout history numerous voices have placed the blame on the woman. For example, the early church father Tertullian writes of Eve:

> You are the devil's gateway: you are the unsealer of that [forbidden tree]; you are the first deserter of the divine law; you are she

who persuaded him whom the devil was not valiant enough to attack. You destroyed God's image, man. On account of your desert—that is, death, even the son of God had to die. Why adorn yourself? All the luxury of feminine dress is the baggage [sic] of women in her condemned and dead estate.[1]

This type of male bias is a perversion of the Scriptures that has hurt and dishonored women. Both ate of the fruit and thus sinned together—she took and ate and gave to him and he ate (Gen. 3:6–7). Therefore, both are culpable. Furthermore, Paul, in 1 Timothy 2:14, writes: "And Adam was not the one deceived; it was the woman who was deceived and became a sinner." Satan took advantage of her vulnerability to seduce her spiritually, whereas Adam knew what he was doing. Consequently, God held him primarily responsible for the Fall. As the head or spiritual leader of the relationship, he was responsible for the relationship.

In Romans 5:12, 17–19, Paul writes that sin entered the world through one man, and death through sin, with the result that all men sinned. The term "men" would have to include women, and the term "man" would have to include Eve, or Paul is saying that only men and Adam sinned and that death came to men and Adam only. But he chose to use the term "man" concerning Adam and appears to place the burden on his shoulders as the primary responsible agent.

There's little indication in Genesis 3:6–7 that God held the man responsible. John Sailhammer points out, though, that in the larger context of the first five books of the Old Testament, the law of Moses teaches that the husband is responsible for the vows of his wife. He writes, "In Numbers 30, if the husband hears his wife make a vow and does not speak out, he is responsible for it." Then he says of Adam: "His silence may be a clue as to why the man must bear the responsibility for the actions of his wife."[2] While both Adam and Eve sinned, God places much of the blame on Adam because as the leader of their relationship, he is responsible for their relationship. His silence as a man throughout the seduction was deafening.

SATAN CONTINUES TO TEMPT
MEN AND WOMEN TO DISOBEY GOD

Was Satan's temptation of Adam and Eve through their sexuality an isolated event without consequences? Not only did their fall plunge all mankind into sin, a theological consequence (Rom. 5:12–19), but it has had a long-term effect on what it means to be an authentic woman or man. As a result of the Fall, men and women have a predisposition to repeat the temptation in their own personal relationships. We discover this almost immediately in the lives of certain couples in the book of Genesis, and we see and experience it in our relationships in this contemporary world.

Adam's World

The temptation of Adam and Eve in Genesis 3 is the proverbial rock that drops in the middle of the pond. As the ripples move out from the initial splash, they adversely affect all who are in their path. The pattern of Eve's controlling initiative and Adam's failure to lead has long-term consequences that, as the book of Genesis graphically portrays, quickly surface in the lives of their descendants. We will eavesdrop on the relationships of two couples: Abraham and Sarah, and Rachel and Jacob.

The Temptation of Abraham and Sarah

When the author of Genesis first introduces us to the family of Sarah and Abraham, he drops a hint of what is to come in Genesis 11:30: "Now Sarai [Sarah] was barren; she had no children." The same will be true for Rebekah and Rachel. In that culture, people believed that children were a blessing from God (Gen. 1:28). Children were very important, especially boys, because large families meant survival in an economy based on the rigors of farming and the herding of cattle. Children also helped protect their families from their enemies. A husband expected his wife to bear him children—lots of them. Psalm 127:3–5 says: "Sons are a heritage from the Lord, children a reward from him. Like arrows in the hands of a warrior are sons born in one's youth. Blessed is the man whose quiver is full of them. They will not be put to shame when they contend with their enemies in the gate." Consequently, a man without children missed a vital part of God's blessing. And a woman who was barren for whatever reason considered herself cursed of God. God had closed up her womb and must be displeased with her.

Genesis 11:29 states in rapid-fire succession that Abraham and his brother married, and that Abraham's wife, Sarah, was barren. Here are a man and a woman who begin their relationship facing a gigantic dilemma. She can't give him something they both want very badly—children. How will those in the community view Abraham as a man? What questions might they ask about his manhood? What questions is he asking about his own manhood? What about the anguish Sarah must feel? An aspect of her womanhood is at issue. How will their community, even their own family, view her as a woman? Most important, how will she view herself? What will both of them think and feel, what will stir within as they watch others celebrate and enjoy their families?

In Genesis 12, however, God speaks to Abraham and much to his delight promises to bless him in many ways, one of which is offspring. Ross writes, "God would give Abram fame and fertility. Here the promise of blessing counteracts the crisis of Sarai's barrenness (11:30)."[3] This would mean a new beginning for both of them. What many considered a curse, God was about to turn to a blessing. The future looked bright for them. They would be able to hold their heads high as they participated in their community—they would be parents, there would be children. God had promised, it would only be a matter of time even though Abraham was now seventy-five years old.

As Adam and Eve were tempted in their sexuality,
so were Abraham and Sarah. Both patterns
are very similar.

Yet nothing happened! The reader of these chapters can feel the tension mounting over the delay as Abraham and Sarah desperately cling to God's promise. In Genesis 15 Abraham expresses his exasperation and impatience to God: "You have given me no children; so a servant in my household will be my heir." But God reiterates his promise to Abraham and confirms it by taking him outside, pointing to the sky, and stating that his offspring would be as innumerable as the stars.

The plot thickens in Genesis 16 as Sarah, still very much barren, begins to yield to temptation and to lose hope and faith in God's promise. She turns instead to her own devices in a last attempt to have a child. Verse 1 begins with a brief, stark reminder of her condition: "Now Sarai, Abram's wife, had borne him no children." So she devises a desperate plan to force the issue in an attempt to satisfy one of the deepest desires of her heart. She approaches Abraham and complains, "The Lord has kept me from having children." Her frustration, and perhaps his, is evident. On the one hand, God has made them a promise, and, on the other, he has kept Sarah barren. It's a contradiction; it simply doesn't make sense. What kind of God would do this? Certainly Sarah would be justified in taking matters into her own hands. Perhaps God was waiting for them to act anyway.

Sarah divulges her plan to Abraham: "Go, sleep with my maidservant; perhaps I can build a family through her." Instead of saying "No, God will do as he promised," he cooperates with her. The plan works, but it turns sour when Hagar, Sarah's pregnant maidservant, turns haughty and begins to despise Sarah as the result of being pregnant (v. 4). In frustration, Sarah turns on Abraham and blames him. Wanting to be free from the situation, Abraham puts Hagar's future in the abusive hands of Sarah (v. 6).

There are many parallels between this temptation and that of Adam and Eve in Genesis 3:1–5 (see fig. 1). For example, Sarah's barren situation places her in a position of great temptation—whether or not to take God at his word. God's word to Adam and Eve was not to eat of the tree of the knowledge of good and evil (Gen. 2:17). All they had to do was trust him. They came to a point, however, when under temptation they stopped trusting God and sought to take control of their own destiny. God had promised Abraham and Sarah a son, but when tempted, they stopped trusting God and took control like their ancestors, Adam and Eve.

ADAM & EVE Genesis 3	ABRAM & SARAI Genesis 16	RACHEL & JACOB Genesis 30
Gen. 3:2 "The woman [Eve] said to"	*Gen. 16:2* "so she [Sarai] said to"	*Gen. 30:1* "so she [Rachel] said to"
Gen. 3:6 "she [Eve] took some"	*Gen. 16:3* "Sarai . . . took"(Implied)	
Gen. 3:6 "she [Eve] also gave some to her husband [Adam]"	*Gen. 16:3* "and [Sarai] gave her to her husband [Abram]"	*Gen. 30:4* "so she [Rachel] gave him [Jacob]. . . ."
Gen. 3:17 "you [Adam] listened to [Eve]"	*Gen. 16:2* "Abram listened to Sarai"(Implied)	

Most important to this book, as Adam and Eve were tempted in their sexuality, so were Abraham and Sarah. Both patterns are very similar. I've displayed several parallels in the first two columns in figure 1. First, just as Eve spoke when she should have waited (Gen. 3:2), so Sarah followed in her footsteps (Gen. 16:2). Both essentially took control of their circumstances. Next, rather than waiting for their husbands to take some initiative and intervened, both of these women became proactive—they took and gave. Eve took some fruit and gave it to Adam (Gen. 3:6), whereas Sarah took Hagar and gave her to Abraham (Gen. 16:3). We're amazed at the control of these women and the relational weakness of these men.

Finally, just as Adam was listening when he should have been leading (Gen. 3:17), so Abraham listened to Sarah when he should have led her (Gen. 16:2). Both men could have said no. They instead became passive. There's a tendency among men to become passive when they don't know what to do in a given situation. Their palms get sweaty, they feel a lump in their throats, and they shift into neutral. Here, both Adam and Abraham knew what God expected, and yet they chose to disobey him rather than trust his word. Rather than look out for God's truth, both conveniently forgot his truth and looked out for themselves. They cooperated with their wives and followed their lead because they wanted to.

The Temptation of Rachel and Jacob

In Genesis 30, Rachel finds herself in the same situation as Sarah and Rebekah before her. Verse 1 says: "When Rachel saw that she was not bearing Jacob any children. . . ." Each of these women experiences an infertility problem that tests to the breaking point her abilities to trust God and His promise of offspring (Gen. 28:14). In Rachel's case, that she is competing with Jacob's other wife, Leah, who provided Jacob with four sons, serves to further complicate her situation.

Like Eve and Sarah before her, she takes the initiative with her husband and demands that he give her a child (see fig. 1). And, she repeats the familiar pattern of speaking when she should have been waiting and trusting. Considering Jacob's response in verse 2, she may be blaming him for her infertility. Rather than understanding her anguish and showing compassion toward her, he became angry with her and, similar to Adam in Genesis 3:12, shifted the blame to God.

Rachel, however has a plan (v. 3). Sound familiar? Like Eve (Gen.

3:6) and Sarah (Gen. 16:3) before her, she gave to her husband. As Sarah gave her maidservant to Abraham, Rachel follows the same pattern and gives her maidservant to Jacob (v. 4). Does Jacob intervene and exercise the leadership she so desperately needs at this point? Will he be a leader and serve her by resisting her misguided efforts and encouraging her instead to trust God for children and not turn to her own devices? By now we know what to expect from these men, and Jacob doesn't disappoint us. Sure enough, in verse 4 he becomes passive and lets her have her own way with him. He lacks responsibility. She has failed him, and he responds by failing her.

Our World

As we observe our own relationships as men and women and those of others around us, we realize that things haven't changed much over the years. What was true in that century remains true in the twenty-first century. Not only was the Eden story reenacted in the book of Genesis, but it's reenacted daily in our modern times.

The Female Temptation. The constant temptation for the female is to take charge of her own life and her relationship with a male. This was Carol's problem in her relationship with men before she met Randy, and it became a primary problem in their relationship after she married Randy. Carol's early life hints at the essence of the problem. She struggles with her womanhood because no one had treated her, nor loved her, as a woman. Her father, who was supposed to lead their family and love her as his daughter, really only teased her with what proved to be an elusive love and then promptly abandoned her. Her mom never seemed to recover from her husband's rejection and abandonment, and was not emotionally able to be there for her daughter.

> *The constant temptation for the female is to take charge of her own life and her relationship with a male.*

None of this, however, prevented Carol from searching for someone to love her. Actually, most women spend much of their lives looking for someone, a man, to love, protect, and honor them. Carol was a very attractive young lady and her high school and college years were characterized by numerous dates. Yet when someone, anyone, got too close, she would feel a growing, numbing pain take charge of the relationship, and push him away, secretly fearing his rejection and eventual abandonment. Thus she was involved in no sustained relationships with men.

Like Carol, many women today have never felt truly loved. Fathers, boyfriends, and husbands haven't been able to deliver. Relationships that began with promise have a way of turning sour over time and not delivering as anticipated. Women vacillate between their disappointments with men and the frightening suspicion that maybe they're not loved because something is wrong with them and they're not worth loving. This is an issue of self-esteem. The ensuing problem of either option is pain. The solution for most women, however, is control. They reason: If I take control of the relationship, or at least if I take responsibility for myself, then I can prevent him from hurting me and possibly, in time, lead him to meet some of the deep longings of my heart.

The Male Temptation. The constant temptation for men is to avoid their responsibility for leadership in their relationships with women. Adam, Abraham, and Jacob abdicated their functions of responsible leadership. This is Randy's struggle as well. As he wrestles with his competence as a man, Carol has begun to press him in ways that frighten him. He believes that he's responsible to lead in their relationship, yet as a relatively new husband he finds himself paralyzed by indecision. He's not sure what to do, so his tendency is to do nothing. Carol, however, seems to have an intuitive awareness of what to do and presses him to respond accordingly. He has begun to resent the pressure, and so he purposely drags his heels.

The constant temptation for men is to avoid their responsibility for leadership in their relationships with women.

Today, far too many men, like Randy, are passive with women who want them to take more initiative in their relationships. They're silent when they should be speaking; they are passive when they should be leading. There is within many men a predisposition to remain quiet when they don't know what to do. And for numerous reasons, men don't know what to do in a relationship with a woman.

Because so many men don't understand women, they find them both fascinating and frightening. On the one hand, a man's ignorance attracts him to a woman. She's so different from him in so many ways that initially he finds himself strangely attracted to her. He's curious about exploring those differences, discovering what makes her tick, and why she makes him feel the way he does when he's around her. On the other hand, a man's ignorance of a woman frightens him. As he enters into a relationship with a woman, he's caught off guard by the moves she makes. He may wonder, How do I relate to this person on an emotional, intimate level? Or she may seem too controlling. For him this is frightening, and his response is to distance himself either emotionally and/or physically. Later, he regains his composure and sense of control and either attempts to reestablish the relationship or looks for a new one.

DISCUSSION QUESTIONS

1. If Satan felt that it was important to tempt Adam and Eve in their sexuality, isn't it likely that he would attack you and your spouse or girlfriend/boyfriend in the same way? What advantage would he gain in your relationship by doing this? Who in your relationship is spiritually responsible to see that this doesn't happen?

2. What have you learned in Genesis 3 about how Satan might go about tempting you and your spouse? Is there any reason why he wouldn't circumvent the man and target the woman? Why would he take this approach?

3. What questions do you have about the character of God? Do you ever feel that God is being unfair to you or is withholding something good from you? Do you believe that God can be trusted? Do you ever doubt his goodness? According to Genesis 3, where might these questions, though legitimate, be coming from?

4. Do you as a woman ever feel tempted like Eve to take charge of

your relationship with men? Is this always wrong? Why or why not? Who is the responsible leader or primary spokesperson in your relationship? Do you find yourself with complete responsibility for the relationship at present? Explain your situation. How does this make you feel? What do you plan to do about it? Why?

5. Do you as a man ever feel tempted to let a woman take charge of your relationship? Do you find that a woman is in charge of your relationship at present? Explain your situation. Do you find it easier to be passive with a woman? How does this make you feel as a man? What do you plan to do about it? Why?

6. Who in the family is spiritually responsible for the relationship? Whom does God hold responsible? Who has taken responsibility in your relationship? Why?

7. Have there been times in your marriage when you can identify with the experience of Abraham and Sarah or Jacob and Rachel? If yes, explain. How did the situation turn out? How might you respond differently if/when it happens again?

Notes

1. Tertullian, *De cultu feminarum* I. 4. I, II. 5 in Jean La Porte, *The Role of Women in Early Christianity* (Lewiston, N.Y.: The Edwin Mellen Press, 1982), p. 27.

2. John H. Sailhammer, *The Pentateuch as Narrative* (Grand Rapids: Zondervan Publishing House, 1992), p. 105.

3. Allen P. Ross, *Creation & Blessing: A Guide to the Study and Exposition of Genesis* (Grand Rapids: Baker Book House, 1988), p. 263.

4

The Fall of Human Sexuality
I Was a Victim!

The Fasten Your Seat Belts sign blinked on as the jet liner began to erratically shake, jerk, and bounce up and down in the bright blue sky over Southern California. In unison, a number of the passengers instinctively turned their heads and looked out the windows to see what was wrong. The pilot was quick to come on the air and announce that the plane was not in any serious jeopardy but was passing through some turbulence, and he asked that everyone please stay seated with their seat belts on until they were past the problem. Randy thought that it felt as if some giant baby boy had the plane in his grasp and was laughing and playing with it like a toy.

Like the plane, Randy and Carol's marriage, like many marriages, was passing through a period of turbulence. An occasional relational shake, jerk, and bounce had gotten their attention. In particular, Carol complained that Randy was not intimate with her. When she told him that, Randy found that he was confused—he didn't understand what she meant. For much of his life and his short marriage, he had associated intimacy with sex. Yet he knew Carol didn't connect the two. Certainly, intimacy included their sexual relationship, but it included more, much more.

As Genesis 3:1–5 portrays the temptation of Adam and Eve, Genesis 3:6–13 presents their fall. In verse 6, the first couple eat of the forbidden fruit and fall. And just as the Temptation has much to do with who they are as a man and a woman, so does their fall. We can't divorce who they are from what they do. In verses 6–13, Adam and

Eve in their sexuality fall and violate their intimacy both with God and themselves. Consequently, this chapter of Genesis falls into two movements. In verses 6–10 we see the vertical dimension of their sin and how sin affected their relationship with their loving Creator. Then in verses 11–13, we see the horizontal dimension of their fall, and how sin affected their relationship with one another. Both have everything to do with intimacy—intimacy between them and God and intimacy between Adam and Eve.

THE SHAME GAME

Genesis 3:6–10 introduces us to the vertical dimension of the Fall by showing how the couple's sin affected their relationship with their sovereign God. Essentially, Adam and Eve fell and lost their intimacy with God. I call this section of Genesis the "shame game." It and the next section compare to a scene in a courtroom. God appears as the skillful prosecutor who asks all the right questions. Adam and Eve are the desperate defendants who, in an attempt to defend themselves, merely incriminate themselves. And the entire episode moves from bad to worse.

Adam and Eve Choose to Eat and Disobey God

Genesis 3:6 records Eve's thoughts and actions during the last few moments before the Fall: "When the woman saw that the fruit of the tree was good for food and pleasing to the eye, and also desirable for gaining wisdom, she took some and ate it." She must have thought that not only can I eat this fruit and it will nourish my body, but it looks good as well. Those in the restaurant business know the importance of making good food look good. One of the appeals of the cafeteria approach to dining is seeing the food before ordering so that diners know what they're getting. Also, the visual experience may cause diners to buy more than they would if ordering from a menu. Some food, such as cabbage or potatoes, though nutritionally sound, is not very appealing to the eye. But it's amazing what a dash of green parsley can do for white potatoes or a serving of orange carrots for grayish-green cabbage when placed next to it.

For Eve there was icing on her cake. Not only did the fruit look good as well as feed her, but it would make her wise. Knowledge, and in particular the wisdom one gains from that knowledge, is power. This is why there is so much emphasis today in our culture on information. We call this the Information Age. Information brings us knowledge that, in turn, can bring us wisdom. Information and wisdom serve to supply us with the necessary power we need to be in control of our lives. Once we're in control, then we are like God. In fact, we really don't need God, we can be our own god. For Eve, the potential for that kind of power was not only irresistible, but it must have been intoxicating.

> *Like a naive teenager buying his first car from a slick, experienced used car salesman, Adam was already convinced and ready to buy, and he would pay dearly for it.*

In the rest of verse 6, Eve initiates and gives to her husband, and he responds and eats of the forbidden fruit. The account is short and seems to move rapidly. With little thought, he follows her leadership and abdicates his own. Adam has heard Satan's "temptation pitch" because he was with Eve throughout the temptation (v. 6). Like a naive teenager buying his first car from a slick, experienced used car salesman, Adam was easily convinced and ready to buy, and paid dearly for it. Both sinned and both fell. First, Eve sinned and then Adam. Both violated their male and female roles and will never fully recover from it.

Adam and Eve's Disobedience Has Dire Consequences

You can't disobey God and expect to get away with it (Hab. 1:13). Sin always has its consequences whether in this life (Deut. 32:35) or the life to come (Rev. 20:11–15). While it may appear that some people get away with evil, ultimately no one gets away with anything. God doesn't wink at sin. The sin and fall of Adam and Eve had several immediate dire consequences (vv. 7–13) as well as long-term consequences (vv. 14–19).

THEY EXPERIENCE AN OVERWHELMING SENSE OF SHAME

The first immediate consequence of their fall is shame. Verse 7 begins with the statement: "Then the eyes of both of them were opened . . ." When the woman ate, she sinned but her eyes were not immediately opened. There was no immediate sense of shame or an awareness of what she had done. When he ate, however, both their eyes were opened and both were aware of their sin and shame. Also, both the man and the woman heard God in the Garden and both hid (v. 8), but God initially addressed Adam in the conversation that followed (vv. 9–11). This would seem to suggest that God waited until Adam ate and then specifically quizzed him because He viewed Adam as the leader and the responsible party for their relationship.

Verse 7 continues: "Then the eyes of both of them were opened, and they realized they were naked; so they sewed fig leaves together and made coverings for themselves." They experienced a tremendous sense of shame as they saw and discovered that they were naked. Apparently, before the Fall they didn't realize that they were naked—they didn't know what naked was. The implication from Genesis 2:25 is now they know that they are naked, and along with that knowledge is an overwhelming sense of shame they had never before experienced. They desired knowledge, but it wasn't the kind of knowledge they had anticipated. They gained what they didn't have before—a knowledge of good and evil (v. 5). They discovered that not only were they not like God, but—to the contrary—they were fundamentally deficient in themselves. They saw themselves as so deeply flawed that they probably questioned their worth as persons.

Shame, like sorrow or anger, can be a very painful emotion. It makes a person want to hide.

Had we been there and asked the man and the woman how they felt, each would have responded: "I feel rotten inside. I'm both angry and resentful [for being found out] and scared. I feel so stupid and worthless as a person. I'm also embarrassed about what I've done, and I don't want anyone to find out about it." Shame, like sorrow or anger, can be a very painful emotion. It makes a person want to hide. This is why Adam and Eve first clothed themselves with fig leaves (v. 7) and then attempted to hide from God (v. 8); they felt so exposed in their nakedness and rebellion. They went their way, not God's way. The problem is that often shame, unlike guilt, leaves a person feeling so flawed that they have little hope of recovery. In extreme cases they ask, "Why would anyone love or care about me, I'm not worth loving."

THEIR INTIMACY WITH GOD
IS REPLACED BY A FEAR OF GOD

A second immediate consequence of their sin is fear. From the time of their creation to the Fall, Adam and Eve knew no fear. We don't know how long this was. Ross suggests: "There is no indication in the narratives of Genesis of long delays between events. It appears that the temptation and fall occurred immediately after Adam and Eve's being created and placed in the garden. . . ."[1] Whatever the time frame, their relationship with God had been on an intimate level. Verse 8 states that Adam and Eve heard the sound of God as He walked in the Garden. How did they know it was the sound of God? I believe that they had heard that sound before and simply recognized who it was. This would suggest that Adam and Eve had spent some time (though limited) with God in the Garden before the Fall. Consequently, they knew God intimately.

Sin had turned Adam's love for God into a fear of God, and so the natural thing for him to do was to hide from the one he feared.

I believe that their intimacy with God was void of any superficiality. The relationship was one of spiritual depth. God is a spirit, so they knew Him in spirit and truth (John 4:24). He initiated a relationship with them and appeared for them in the garden, demonstrating His approachability and openness. They experienced his sensitivity, tender strength, gentleness, kindness, authenticity, as well as His other attributes. Certainly they knew Him as did Moses in Exodus 34:6–7 who, based on his experience with God, described him as compassionate, gracious, abounding in love, and faithful.

Whereas before the Fall Adam and Eve must have eagerly anticipated intimacy with their Creator, verse 8 says that this time they hid from God among the trees in the Garden. Why did they hide from God? When God calls for a response, Adam explains in verse 10: "I heard you in the garden, and I was afraid because I was naked; so I hid." Sin had turned Adam's love for God into a fear of God, and so the natural thing for him to do was to hide from the One he feared. Also, Adam knew that, according to Genesis 2:17, God would punish him with death. John sums it up well in 1 John 4:18: "There is no fear in love. But perfect love drives out fear, because fear has to do with punishment. The one who fears is not made perfect in love."

The process of Adam and Eve's sin is instructive. It progresses from shame to fear and concludes with hiding. It is a downward spiral (fig. 1). First, they eat, their eyes are opened, and they realize to some degree what they've done; they've sinned against the Creator God of the universe. This brings an overwhelming sense of shame. Then that shame and its consequence—a feeling of exposure—leads to fear. Whereas before the Fall they loved and enjoyed their Creator because of who He is, now they fear Him. But they have reason to fear Him because they have disobeyed and rebelled against Him. Again, disobedience has its consequences. Finally, the shame and the fear naturally led to a vain attempt to hide from the God who is the only solution to their dilemma. From the Fall on, all of us will find in sin a sense of shame and exposure accompanied by fear and a desire to hide from God.

SHAME

FEAR

HIDING

(Figure 1)

THEY NO LONGER FULLY REFLECT GOD'S IMAGE

We learned in Genesis 1 that God created Adam and Eve in his image (vv. 26–27). While they expressed God's image in many ways, one way was to reflect God's to one another and back to God. For example, as God loved and cared, so they loved and cared for one another and God. Now the question is, What effect did the Fall have on the image of God as expressed in Adam and Eve?

The New Testament provides evidence that the Fall marred the image of God in Adam and Eve but it didn't eradicate that image altogether. Ryrie writes: "One may say it was defaced though not erased."[2] In 1 Corinthians 11:7, well after the Fall, Paul encourages the men in the church at Corinth not to cover their heads in worship because a man is "the image and glory of God." And in James 3:9, James writes that we can use our tongues for contradictory purposes— to praise God or to curse men. Then of the men he says that they "have been made in God's likeness." Ryrie correctly observes that: "These passages would have no basis if the image had been erased in the Fall."[3]

Another question is, What does the change in image mean? It means that the first couple will no longer reflect or mirror his attributes as in the Garden. Though they'll continue to mirror God's image, it won't be the same. Figure 2 shows how Adam and Eve reflected God's image before the Fall and how they reflected His image after the Fall.

BEFORE THE FALL	AFTER THE FALL
Sensitivity	Insensitivity
Integrity	Infidelity
Strength	Weakness
Tenderness	Callousness
Trust	Suspicion
Caring	Neglecting
Unconditional Love	Conditional Love
Honesty	Deception
Closeness	Distance

(Figure 2)

Sometimes Adam and Eve and their children will mirror the characteristics on the left side of figure 3. At other times, however, they will mirror those on the right side. Much of the time, however, the right side will dominate the left side. People will tend to love others conditionally before they'll love them unconditionally. While some people are sensitive, most tend to be insensitive. We naturally move to the right side, not the left (Rom. 7:14–25), and that's the problem.

Here's an illustration to compare what life was like before and then after the Fall of man. When people buy a new car, they like to park it away from the other cars. At shopping centers these cars are like isolated islands afloat in a vast, empty sea of concrete, parked all by themselves a great distance from the buildings. By doing this, new car owners hope that no one will park next to them and mar the brand-new paint job by opening a car door into the side of their new car. Once the new acrylic paint on a car is marred, it will never be the same. Not only will the car decrease in value, but the door has lost an element of its original beauty. While it's true that you can repaint the blemished door, over time the touched-up area fades in contrast to the original paint.

Likewise, after the Fall, the full enjoyment of manhood and womanhood won't be the same. While living in the garden, Adam and Eve mirrored the left side of figure 2. In their relationship, they lived and experienced sensitivity, unconditional love, and the other divine attributes that God shares with humanity. From the Fall on, Adam and Eve and all their descendants will live and experience both sides of figure 2. In their courtship, most couples spend more time reflecting the left side to each other. They tend to be at their best for their potential life's partner. This serves only to heighten expectations for both of them of the marriage relationship. After marriage when the honeymoon is over, the couple settles down and begins to experience both sides of figure 2. The result is that neither partner essentially meets the other's expectations.

THE BLAME GAME

Whereas in Genesis 3:6–10 Adam and Eve fell and lost their intimacy with God, in verses 11–13 they lost their intimacy with one another. Genesis 3:6–10 represents the vertical dimension of the Fall and how it affected their intimacy with God. Verses 11–13 present the horizontal relationship and how the Fall affected their intimacy with each another. By the time we reach verse 11, Adam and Eve are no longer completing one another as God had originally intended (1 Cor. 11:11–12), but they are competing with one another as both become ensnared in the "blame game" as the result of God's probing questions.

Adam Blames the Fall on Eve and God

Beginning in verse 9 and stretching through verse 13, God becomes a skillful prosecuting attorney and probes both Adam and the woman with penetrating questions to force them to face what they've done. In verse 11 God probes Adam with a question to which he doesn't expect an answer: "Who told you that you were naked? Have you eaten from the tree that I commanded you not to eat from?" God obviously knows what Adam has done, and Adam realizes that with God's question. Adam knows he's been found out in spite of his futile attempts at covering up his shame and exposure with fig leaves and his attempt to hide from God.

Not only does God want Adam to acknowledge his sin, he is giving Adam a chance to recover from his wrong and a second chance to be a man with Eve. Verse 11, therefore, represents grace and potential forgiveness. In verse 8 Adam and Eve heard the sound of God as he was walking in the garden. According to one writer, the expression "the sound of the Lord God" is a common expression found in the first five books of the Old Testament (especially in Deut.—see 5:25; 8:20; 13:19; 15:5; 18:16; and 26:14) and means God's call to obedience. Sailhammer writes: "It can hardly be without purpose that the author opens the scene of the curse with a subtle but painful reminder of the single requirement for obtaining God's blessing: 'to hear/obey the voice of the Lord God.'"[4]

Here was an opportunity for Adam to acknowledge his failure and incompetence as a man regarding the Fall. He could take responsibility for what he had done as the leader, and he could ask God for forgiveness based on his grace. God is inviting Adam to take some initiative and come clean—to tell the truth and confess his sin. This is an invitation to renew a right relationship with his God. It is also an invitation to be a leader in his relationship with Eve; an invitation, in short, be a man. But in verse 12, we see that Adam fails, and in doing so, he fails Eve again.

Here was an opportunity for Adam to acknowledge his failure and incompetence as a man regarding the Fall.

Adam's reply in verse 12 acknowledges his guilt but attempts to shift much of the blame to Eve and ultimately God, Himself. Adam responds to God's probing: "The woman you put here with me—she gave me some fruit from the tree, and I ate it. What was I to do? It was her fault! Had she not initiated and given me the fruit, it would have never happened." The latter part of the verse, "and I ate it," seems only a natural consequence—something that any red-blooded man would have done.

In Adam's reply there is also the subtle reminder that God supplied the woman for Adam; it was all God's idea. He takes God's act of blessing and grace in supplying what was missing in Adam's life— the woman as a helper—and attempts to use it to place some of the blame on God. After all, if God hadn't created Eve and brought her to Adam, this would never have happened. Adam treats God's blessing as a curse. This reasoning is like a driver blaming General Motors for a careless accident one has while driving a Chevrolet. Adam has a bad case of victimitis. He's saying that he's a victim in this tragedy and not a blameworthy agent.

Eve Blames the Fall on the Serpent

Eve doesn't respond any better than Adam. In verse 12, God probes her and she responds: "The serpent deceived me, and I ate." Just as God has graciously given Adam a second chance, so he's giving Eve a second chance as well. The question is, Will she accept responsibility for her part in the Fall? Will she, unlike Adam, acknowledge her failure, confess it as sin, and ask her holy God for his forgiveness? Will she acknowledge her failure as a woman and begin to act as a supportive helper to Adam? But Eve, too, has a case of "victimitis." What she answers is true, however, it doesn't go far enough. Eve sees herself as a blameless victim of the serpent rather than one who should have turned to her husband during the temptation.

Eve sees herself as a blameless victim of the serpent rather than one who should have deferred to her husband during the temptation.

From here on, Adam and Eve's relationship will never be the same. They have violated their intimacy with one another. Alienation and mistrust have replaced the intimacy they had once known. Genesis 2:25 presents the intimacy they had with each other under true headship before the Fall: "The man and his wife were both naked, and they felt no shame." Not only were they naked physically, but they were naked emotionally. Although the verse doesn't say it, I believe that they shared an openness to communicate with one another at a deeper level, that they could talk freely about things that were important to both of them—the things that really mattered regardless of how insignificant. They could talk about the issues of the heart such as their attitudes, longings, feelings, and deepest needs. They communicated with insight and with sensitivity to the other's ideas. In doing so they were extremely vulnerable but were willing to take the risk because they felt no shame. There was no need to cover up—to protect oneself emotionally from the other partner.

Throughout the following verses, and for the rest of their lives, the first couple—and all couples as their descendants, including Randy and Carol—will struggle with intimacy. While it will still be possible for men and women to be emotionally intimate with one another since the Fall, it won't be easy. Men like Randy will interpret and mistakenly associate intimacy with sex and limit it primarily to the physical act of sex. This, in turn, will serve to anger and frustrate women like Carol. Should wives in anger choose not to respond to their husbands' sexual advances, their husbands will react by withdrawing from them so that there's little, if any, intimacy in the ensuing relationship. Consequently, wives become starved for intimacy and look for it in another (a child, a parent, a good female friend, or a male lover) or become cold and callous toward their husbands, convinced that they can survive without their husband's intimacy.

While it will still be possible for men and women to be emotionally intimate with one another since the Fall, it won't be easy.

Carol and Randy are not yet at this point so early in their marriage. Yet both have begun to sense that they aren't experiencing the kind of intimacy in their relationship that God intended. The problem, as in most relationships, begins with the man. Randy doesn't really understand emotional intimacy. It's highly probable that before they married he was emotionally intimate with Carol. They had agreed not to become sexually involved before marriage, and so he spent much time communicating with, and listening to, Carol.

Randy felt free to share with Carol certain issues of the heart, and she shared the same with him. He told her what it was like growing up in his family and about the deep feelings and longings that were stored up inside him. He also shared with her his anger at this dad and his struggles with feelings of incompetence and inadequacy as a man. He didn't want to grow up to be like his father who proved so impotent. Yet except for a coach or two, his dad was the only model Randy ever knew. He hoped that God would help him, and that he wouldn't turn out to be the same kind of husband and father as his dad.

Carol shared with Randy her feelings toward her dad and how she feared that someday Randy might abandon her. She also talked about her need for strong emotional, spiritual involvement from others, especially Randy, and how she struggled with feelings of low self-esteem. Most important to her, Randy spoke with insight and listened with sensitivity—he seemed to resonate with an innate understanding of Carol. Randy didn't realize, however, that he was being intimate and how important that was to her. He took that part of their premarital relationship for granted, and after they married, he pursued sex as a substitute for intimacy. Carol didn't understand the change in Randy and assumed that something had gone wrong in the relationship. It was beginning to bother her to the point that it became an issue. If something didn't change, the marriage would be in deep trouble in another three to five years.

DISCUSSION QUESTIONS

1. In general, do you want to be aware of what is going on around you? If yes, do you know why? Do you like to feel that you're in control of your life? How do you feel when you think that you're in control? If someone offered you the opportunity to control your own life and destiny, would you be interested? Why or why not?

2. Most people wince at the idea of being seen physically naked. Why do people react that way? Does it have anything to do with Adam and Eve and the Fall? Most people are reluctant to expose themselves emotionally as well. Why? Does this reluctance have anything to do with the Fall?

3. How do you feel when you've sinned? Do you ever feel ashamed? If yes, describe what it feels like. Is that shame ever accompanied by the fear of exposure—the fear that others will find out what you've done and devalue or reject you as a person? If this is the case, do you react by trying to hide what you've done? Why? Does this sound like Adam and Eve's experience in the Fall? Have you ever felt so ashamed of yourself that you're convinced there's no hope for you?

4. When you first meet people, especially the opposite sex, do you tend to be at your best behavior? Why or why not? Do you think this affects the long term expectations of that person? Do you find that you're at your best behavior in a relationship with a person, especially the opposite sex or a spouse, over an extended time such as six months, a year, or two years? Why or why not? What might this have to do with the Fall and its impact on the image of God in us?

5. How easy is it for you to accept responsibility when you do something wrong? Is your natural tendency to blame yourself or someone else? How might you explain this? Do you ever blame God? Like Adam and Eve, do you ever feel like a victim? Is this a legitimate feeling? Were Adam and Eve victims? Were they responsible victims?

6. How do you normally respond when someone accuses you of wrongdoing? How do you respond when you know they're correct? Do you ever use a true accusation against you as an opportunity to right a wrong? Why or why not?

7. If you're a man, how do you define intimacy? If you're a woman, how would you define intimacy? Often men and women define intimacy differently. What are some of those differences? Is physical sex related to intimacy? Why or why not?

8. Are you ever intimate with God? Explain. Is there a difference between being intimate with the opposite sex and with God? If yes, what is the difference? How has the Fall affected intimacy with God and intimacy between a man and a woman? Is this true in your life?

Notes

1. Allen P. Ross, *Creation & Blessing: A Guide to the Study and Exposition of Genesis* (Grand Rapids: Baker Book House, 1988), p. 143.

2. Charles C. Ryrie, *Basic Theology: A Popular Systematic Guide to Understanding Biblical Truth* (Wheaton, Ill.: Victor Books, 1986), p. 192.

3. Ibid.

4. John H. Sailhammer, *The Pentateuch as Narrative* (Grand Rapids: Zondervan Publishing House, 1992), p. 105.

The Judgment of Human Sexuality
Guilty As Charged

The spacious Boeing 747 nosed out over the Pacific Ocean, and the cabin grew quiet as almost everyone settled down for the long flight to Hawaii. The turbulence had subsided, and the captain had promised to hold any announcements to a minimum so that the passengers could have an uninterrupted period of leisure. Some read their paperback novels, or tourist brochures describing the allure of Hawaii. Several tapped away at the keys on their laptop computers. Some slept while others with headsets in place listened to music ranging from Mozart to Grunge. After serving a light snack of ham sandwiches and potato chips along with a favorite beverage, the flight attendants settled down either at the front or the rear of the cabin. The only obvious movement was a solo flight attendant periodically checking on people's needs, or an occasional passenger navigating the aisles in search of a bathroom.

Randy and Carol had selected two adjacent seats next to a window. The Boeing 747 is a large plane with seats located by the windows on either side and down the center of the plane. Two aisles, a left one and a right one, separate the seats by the windows from those in the center. Carol preferred the seat immediately next to the window, while Randy intentionally chose the seat on the left aisle so he could stretch out his long legs.

Carol tilted the back of her seat the maximum six to eight inches, loosened her seatbelt, closed her eyes, and appeared to be napping. But her excitement over this, her first trip to Hawaii, wouldn't allow her to doze off. As she reclined there, her scattered thoughts turned to conversations with Randy over their marriage. He had expressed deep concern over what he felt was Carol's attempts to control him in the marriage. While he had trouble articulating exactly what he meant, he cited several examples to illustrate his concern. Some had to do with her anger. There were occasions when they didn't agree on some issue, so she would get mad and not speak to him for a day or two. She claimed that he hurt her feelings; he felt manipulated. Though Carol and Randy viewed these situations differently, she knew from their premarital counseling and her earlier relationships with other men that she had some problem in this area. Their counselor at Fellowship Church suggested that it might have something to do with the early abandonment by her dad. Carol would eventually learn that it went back a lot further than that.

Randy attempted to distribute his wiry 6' 2" frame in the cramped space between his seat and the one in front. He was most comfortable when he spread his legs out into the aisle. The only problem was that he had to remain alert to the passing traffic. Passengers navigating the aisles might not see him and trip over his legs or feet. Also, when the attendants wheeled their food and beverage cart down the aisle, he stood the chance of getting his legs bruised. What all this activity meant to this light sleeper was that he could either relax and nod off, thereby risking bodily harm, or he could stay awake and be mildly comfortable. He opted for the latter, and, like Carol, his thoughts turned to his feelings about himself and his marriage.

In the conversations that followed their infrequent quarrels, most of her complaints could be traced back to his initial passivity. She wanted him to assert himself more and to show some initiative in their relationship, especially in the little things. For example, she wished that he would notice when she was upset or tired and ask what was wrong or offer to help her with some of her responsibilities at home. She also wished he would take her side when she was uspset about something, or that he would tell her that he loved her several times a day. She felt that he had taken a back seat especially in this area of their marriage, and that in doing so he was avoiding his leadership responsibility. In other areas she simply took the initiative because he showed so little. She wondered if maybe that was why he felt controlled, which, if true, wasn't fair to her. After all, this was their marriage, and she couldn't just sit back and watch it drift haphazardly in any direction like a ship with a broken rudder.

Carol's feelings stunned and hurt Randy, and his first reaction was to discount them. To complicate matters, he didn't understand exactly what she meant. The more he thought about her complaints and his inadequacies, his pain subsided and he was willing to acknowledge that there was a problem. He struggled with feelings of incompetence, and he delayed making decisions affecting their marriage because he feared they would be the wrong decisions. Their counselor at Fellowship Church believed that Randy's feelings of incompetence might have something to do with his relationship with his dad. While this had a deep impact on Randy, the problem went a lot further back than his dad, as he was about to discover.

Genesis 3 is a record of the corruption of human sexuality. The process began with a temptation (vv. 1–5) that resulted in the Fall (vv. 6–13). It climaxed with God's judgment (vv. 14–19). God as the prosecuting attorney probed the two defendants who reluctantly admitted some guilt but shifted the blame to others. Now God moves from the role of prosecutor to judge and pronounces final judgment. It is threefold and applies first to the serpent (vv. 14–15), then to the woman (v. 16), and finally to the man (vv. 16–19). His judgment on the serpent (Satan) will be good news for Adam and Eve and their posterity. His judgment on them, however, will be bad news and will affect their posterity (Exod. 34:7). Most important to this chapter, God's judgment is unique both to Adam and Eve and relates specifically to their sexual identity as man and woman.

GOD'S JUDGMENT OF THE SERPENT

In Genesis 3:14–15, God judges the snake and predicts a chain of events that will provide the potential for the redemption of mankind. Therefore, this judgment is good news for Adam and Eve who might be standing near by and listening in on the conversation. God's judgment of the serpent is stronger than that for the man and the woman, for it involves a curse, whereas theirs is a punishment. A judgment involves punishment and says that from here on life will be painful, but for Adam and Eve it includes various positive provisions for relief and victory. A curse includes punishment and pain without any positive provisions.[1] The curse on the serpent was twofold.

God Humbles the Serpent

Initially, God appears to curse the snake for its involvement in the Temptation and Fall. Whereas the snake was crafty in verse 1, now it's cursed. The curse involves humbling the snake; it will now crawl through the dust on the ground in defeat (Isa. 49:23; 65:25). Thus, every time we spot a snake crawling across the ground, it serves as a perpetual reminder of the serpent's role in the Fall of mankind.

It seems strange that God would treat a common serpent in this manner. The passage gives us very little information about the snake and what it was like in its original state. Did the snake look like today's snakes? Did it stand upright? Did God create it so that it could carry on a conversation with the first family? Did it willfully cooperate with Satan in the temptation of the first family? We don't know. God chose not to give us this information. All we know is that God isn't capricious nor unjust and does what is right. In these verses, however, it becomes obvious that the serpent is no mere common garden-variety snake. You would make a grave mistake if you only pictured him as a harmless snake quietly nestled in the flower bed in your back yard.

God Will Defeat Satan

Verse 15 says that God will place enmity between the serpent and Eve and that it will extend to the offspring of both. Ultimately, there will be a final crushing blow that will defeat the serpent, though he'll strike the woman's heel. The New Testament suggests that this describes the perpetual conflict between Satan and his forces (John 8:44) and the woman, Eve, and her seed, culminating in Christ (Rom. 16:20, Rev. 20:7–10). The enmity is a continuation of the cosmic conflict that Christ will eventually win.

Sailhammer comments:

> The snake, the woman, and the man are not depicted as individuals involved in a personal crisis; rather, they are representatives. We are left with the impression that this is not their story as much as it is our story, the story of humankind. With great skill the author has presented these three participants as the heads of their race. The snake on the one hand and the man and the woman on the other are as two great nations embarking on a great struggle, a struggle that will find its conclusion only by an act of some distant and as yet unidentified "seed."[2]

This is *our* story in that the conflict between Eve's seed (us, as her descendants) involves the Cross. When Christ died on the cross, he provided the basis for the redemption of mankind and the ultimate victory over Satan (John 12:31). The Cross, in turn, provides the basis for the redemption of our relationship with God and the relationship between a man and a woman. This good news is a breath of fresh air, in comparison to what has just taken place in the Garden. It is good news for at least two reasons.

> *When Christ died on the cross, he provided the basis for the redemption of mankind and the ultimate victory over Satan.*

First, it's good news because it says that there's hope for mankind in Christ. When Adam sinned, he brought sin and death on all mankind (Rom. 5:12–21). That includes all of us as well as anyone who has ever lived on planet earth. However, Christ's death on the cross accomplished a number of blessings, one of which is the potential for the redemption of all women and men (Matt. 20:28; Gal. 3:13). Consequently, all who trust in Christ's payment for their sins are redeemed from the penalty of their sins—spiritual death. Consequently, in spite of the Fall, we can have a relationship with God through Christ.

Second, it's good news because it says that there's hope for the relationship between a man and a woman. Sin not only drove a relational wedge between the first couple and God, but, as we discovered in verses 7–13, it drove a relational wedge between Adam and Eve and all other couples, as demonstrated by Abraham and Sarah, Rachel and Jacob, and their descendents. Christ's death removed that wedge for all those who accept him. The marriage of two unbelievers, however, still faces that relational wedge. They can relate to one another physically and emotionally, but not spiritually. They are missing the foundation that every marriage needs to survive. Without faith in Christ and a conviction that the Bible is God's word to mankind, anything goes. Christian couples who base their marriage on the Scriptures can have not only a vital connection with Christ, but with one another. Sin doesn't have to be a wedge that drives them apart and ruins their relationship. Sin doesn't have to control their lives and disrupt their relationship with one another (Rom. 6). And it's this vital spiritual dimension that holds the key to what it means to be an authentic woman and man.

GOD'S JUDGMENT ON THE WOMAN

In Genesis 3:16, God judges the woman, Eve. This judgment relates directly to the very core of her unique sexual identity—to Eve as a woman. It affects her sexuality in two different ways. The first relates to her function as a childbearer, and the second to her relationship with the man. Again, we must remember that Eve's story is every woman's story, for what takes place here affects all women throughout history.

The Woman Will Experience Pain in Childbirth

Though Eve has not yet become a mother, that's God's intention for her as a woman. An aspect of her reflecting the image of God according to Genesis 1:28 is bearing children. Toward the end of Genesis 3, Adam prophetically gives her the name Eve, which means "the mother of all living" (v. 20). Consequently, she is the mother of us all. She's a great-great-grandparent, and all of us can trace our ancestry back to her. Adam's prophecy was eventually fulfilled in Genesis 4 with the births of Cain, Abel, and Seth.

God's judgment doesn't negate His plan for Eve to have children. The judgment is that now it will be a very painful experience. That's the bad news. As a childbearer she will experience pain both physically and emotionally.

I'll never know the physical pain that my wife experienced in the births of our four children. She's convinced that the two most painful areas of her life have been childbearing and kidney stones. I had the privilege of being in the delivery room at the birth of our last son. I can remember trying to coach and comfort her as she bore the extreme pain of childbirth. I can also remember carrying her out to the car and rushing her to the hospital because of a sharp, intense pain in her lower back that turned out to be kidney stones.

Bearing children can also involve emotional pain. There may be some emotional pain as a new mother anticipates the intense physical pain and difficulties associated with childbirth. The frequent experience of postpartum depression in women also signals the presence of emotional pain. Finally, what couple, especially the mom, doesn't go through much personal pain as their children grow and develop into adults.

> *God's judgment doesn't negate his plan for Eve to have children. The judgment is that now it will be a very painful experience. That's the bad news.*

All of this pain, whether physical or emotional, serves as a reminder to women in particular of the Fall and God's judgment. Pain is a constant reminder that sin has its consequences. At the same time, however, it's also a sign of God's grace and future blessing. Psalm 127:3–5 says: "Sons are a heritage from the Lord, children a reward from him. Like arrows in the hands of a warrior are sons born in one's youth. Blessed is the man whose quiver is full of them. They will not be put to shame when they contend with their enemies in the gate."

The Woman Will Attempt to Control Her Husband

Besides pain in childbearing, another aspect of the woman's judgment is also found in verse 16. God says to Eve: "Your desire will be for your husband. . . ." What does this mean? Some interpret it to mean that the wife will desire her husband sexually or emotionally. That interpretation doesn't seem to be true to life as many men will affirm.

The solution to interpretation is to look for additional information in the context of the passage. The key term in the verse is desire, and it's used in a similar way in Genesis 4:7 (fig. 1).[3] Genesis 4 begins with the story of Adam's first two sons, Cain and Abel. Both have presented offerings to the Lord, who has accepted Abel's offering and rejected Cain's. Cain became so angry at God that it affected his appearance (v. 6). In verse 7, God says to Cain: "If you do what is right, will you not be accepted? But if you do not do what is right, sin is crouching at your door; it desires to have you, but you must master it."

THE ONGOING STRUGGLE FOR CONTROL

Genesis 3:16
". . . Your [Eve's] desire will be for your husband [Adam], and he [Adam] will rule over you [Eve]."

Genesis 4:7
". . . But if you do not do what is right, sin is crouching at your door; it [sin] desires to have you, but you [Cain] must master it."

(Figure 1)

In verse 7, the term desire seems to have the meaning of enslave, master, or control. The idea is that sin wants to master, subdue, control, take over, or enslave Cain. This seems to be the meaning as well in Genesis 3:16 and would indicate that Eve's desire was to master, control, or subdue Adam. God's judgment on Eve goes something like this: You took control of the relationship during the temptation, and you prompted Adam to eat and sin; consequently, your judgment is that throughout the relationship you'll be looking for opportunities to take control. Eve's constant temptation while living with Adam will be to repeat the Fall, that is, to master, control, or have her own way.

The Husband Will Dominate the Woman

Whereas Eve's desire will be to control her husband, Adam will resist her control, as the last part of verse 15 indicates that it won't work. God says to Eve: "Your desire will be for your husband, and he will rule over you." A third aspect of her judgment, and the down side of her attempt at mastery, is that he'll "stiff arm" her attempts to control him.

The key term in this last part of verse 16 is "rule." Hebrew scholar Allen Ross provides us with an important insight on the meaning of rule in Genesis 3:16:

This word cannot be weakened to mean leadership alone, as many expositors wish to do. It is a term that describes dominion, mastery, lordship. It can have a rather harsh application. The significant point about this verse is that it is part of the punishment oracle for sin. To attempt to make it teach the submission of the

woman to her husband and the loving leadership of the husband
to his wife completely misses the point.[4]

It's also the same term translated "master" in Genesis 4:7 (fig. 1).
God told Cain that because sin is crouching and waiting to take control
of him that his only hope was to master or dominate it. He ignored
this warning, however, so sin took control, and he murdered his brother,
Abel (v. 8).

The idea in Genesis 3:16 is that the man will respond to the woman's
desire to control him by controlling, dominating or mastering her.
He'll not respond positively, but negatively. He'll strongly, even
harshly, resist her attempts to take him over. This is because these
attempts leave him feeling incompetent as a man and emasculated.
Her attempts to control him and attract him will only push him further
away from her. Ultimately, he'll dominate or abuse her emotionally
and physically, and this will serve as a constant reminder to the
generations that follow of the Fall.

*The man will strongly react to the woman's desire to
control him by dominating or mastering her.*

This judgment signals the beginning of male domination, not male
headship. There is a vast difference between biblical male headship
and male domination. The two must never be associated. Male
headship is found in Genesis 2 where God determined that Adam
was to be the woman's head (1 Cor. 11:7–10). This put the
responsibility for their relationship in his hands. He was now
responsible to lead, or serve, Eve. Genesis 2:25 pictures Adam and
Eve's relationship as completely open and transparent. There were
no secrets nor fear of vulnerability. They trusted one another and
experienced a rich intimacy together. That's what it was like to live
under biblical headship. Then male domination enters the picture in
Genesis 3. In verse 16 it all turns ugly. Both partners sin and fall, and
much of what they had is lost. The disastrous consequences are
enormous. Whereas Adam formerly served Eve as her equal partner,
now he'll attempt to enslave her as he asserts dominion over her. In
doing so he serves only to mimic the pagan leadership that Christ so
soundly condemns in Matthew 20:25.

But how will domination affect future generations of men and women in their relationships with one another? Because of this judgment, there will be the predisposition in women to control and men to dominate. This is the classic battle of the sexes that even secular writers have observed to be an inherent part of human history. Ross writes: "Eve is an archetype, that is, if she represents every woman as Adam represents every man, then the story portrays a characteristic of human nature—the woman at her worst would be a nemesis to the man, and the man at his worst would dominate the woman."[5] Eve, in a sense, is the archetype of every woman and does represent them, as Adam is the archetype and represents every man. Whereas God had intended for men and women to complement one another, they have sinned and now the prospect for all men and women is competition with one another.

GOD'S JUDGMENT ON THE MAN

In Genesis 3:17–19, God judges Adam by pronouncing a curse on the ground. As the judgment on Eve affected her at the very core of her sexuality, so this judgment will affect Adam in the same way. God's judgment isn't capricious. Both sinned in the context of their sexuality—his maleness and her femaleness; therefore, both are judged in the same context. As with Eve's judgment, this one is bad news for Adam. The despair of this section of Genesis is best understood in the context of Adam's original creative purpose.

God Created the Man to Rule the World

We discovered in Genesis 1 that God created human sexuality—the man and the woman—to reflect or mirror His image (Gen. 1:26–27). Adam and Eve would accomplish this in a number of ways. As God produced life, so, in time, Adam and Eve would produce life (Gen. 1:28). Reproduction will commence in Genesis 4 as Adam and his wife, Eve, the mother of all living, would bear Cain, Abel, and Seth. In addition, Genesis 5:5 indicates that Adam and Eve had other sons and daughters.

Adam and Eve also reflected God's image by sharing His character and many of His attributes. This included such character qualities as unconditional love, honesty, patience, faithfulness, trustworthiness, sensitivity, integrity, and so on. They reflected these back to God and to one another.

Most important to Adam's judgment, Adam and Eve mirrored God's image by exercising dominion over creation. In Genesis 1:28, God instructed them to fill, subdue, and rule over creation. Then in Genesis 2, God placed Adam in a perfect environment—Paradise (vv. 8–10) with a perfect employment—to work the ground from which he had come and take care of it (vv. 5, 15). The ground in turn would supply him with food and aesthetic pleasure (v. 9).

Adam would experience a strong sense of self-worth and fulfillment. He had no reason to doubt his competence, for creation would respond to his every wish. What he said, it would do.

The impression one gathers from all this is that God blessed Adam with a great life, and that Adam would enjoy living, working, and worshiping in the Garden. The man would experience a sense of great worth and self-fulfillment. He had no reason to doubt his competence, for creation would respond to his every wish. What he said, it would do. The ground must have been pleasurable to work and yielded maximum fruitfulness. He had the world at his fingertips; in essence, he ruled the world.

The World Will Resist Man's Rule

All this changed drastically with the ensuing judgment and curse on the ground in Genesis 3:17–19. As the result of the Fall, it would be very difficult and particularly frustrating to rule the world. What had been most pleasurable would now be most painful. Rather than respond to his efforts to control the world, from here on his world will resist his efforts to rule it. The judgment section in Genesis begins with the reasons for the curse, then presents the curse, and follows with the impact of the curse.

The Reasons for the Curse. In verse 17, God said to Adam: "'Because you listened to your wife and ate from the tree about which I commanded you, 'you must not eat of it,' Cursed is the ground because of you. . . .'" Thus He provides Adam and us with two reasons why He was about to curse the ground. The first had to do with his sexuality—what it meant for Adam to be a man. As we discovered earlier, God is saying to Adam that he should have been leading when he was listening. Rather than intervene, he did nothing. When he should have been proactive, he was passive. He stood by, listened, and made no effort to disrupt the temptation. Thus, he failed to serve Eve as her protector, and he failed himself as a man.

The second had to do with his disobedience to God. He obeyed his wife instead of his God and ate from the tree of the knowledge of good and evil. God didn't hand Adam a long list of dos and don'ts. There was no dirty dozen or nasty nine. And he could eat from, and enjoy, any tree in the garden except one. Adam had only one requirement—don't eat of one specific tree. The issue was whether he would trust the Creator or the creature. Would he obey or disobey? Although Adam attempts to blame God and the woman for his tragic action (v. 12), he knew what he was doing (1 Tim. 2:14).

The Object of the Curse. In verse 17, God pronounces a curse on the ground, which had been a major part of Adam's life. It meant everything to Adam. He was made from it, he worked it, and it provided his food. God didn't curse the man, but the ground to which he would eventually return. But by cursing the ground, in effect, God was judging Adam. The ground affected so much of what he did that whatever happened to the ground happened in some measure to Adam.

The Result of the Curse. The curse affected Adam primarily in the area of the work that would provide his food. God said to the man: "Cursed is the ground because of you; through painful toil you will eat of it all the days of your life. It will produce thorns and thistles for you, and you will eat the plants of the field. By the sweat of your brow you will eat your food until you return to the ground, since from it you were taken; for dust you are and to dust you will return."

Adam's job was to continue to work the ground as it would provide his sustenance. Only it wouldn't be anything like it was before the Fall. It now had pain written all over it. Anyone who has ever worked on a farm before today's modern equipment has some idea of what is ahead for Adam. He'll know what it's like to eke out a living. He'll experience blisters, calluses, and sore muscles. The sun will tan his skin a deep brown as he wipes the sweat from its heat off his brow. And at the end of a hard day's work, extreme fatigue will greet him.

Add to all of this a deep sense of frustration and humiliation. Creation will now resist him. Once his friend, now it will mock and intimidate him. Instead of producing at maximum capacity based on its rich fertility, the infertile ground will strain to produce anything at all. Hard, strenuous work will produce only thorns and thistles. And this will serve as a constant reminder of the Fall.

> *Creation will now resist Adam. Once his friend,*
> *now it will mock and intimidate him.*

Adam will know what it's like to be a failure, and he'll question his competence. This kind of experience is very hard on the male ego. It leaves a man feeling weak and impotent as a man. Most likely, he will focus on areas where he perceives that he's competent and avoid areas of incompetence. There will exist a compulsive desire to win and prove his competence. And he'll repeat this pattern in an attempt to prove to himself and others that he can still cut it as a man. Maybe that will quiet the small voice that keeps whispering in his ear that maybe he really is a loser.

Unfortunately for Adam, this will not be a temporary condition. There's no end in sight. God tells him in verse 17 that this situation "will last all the days of your life." Then someday he'll die and become a part of what he was created from and has worked all his life. The fact that many of life's painful situations are short term gives us hope. Adam's situation, however, is hopeless. He has traded life for death. Instead of being like God, he's like dust—he's frail humanity, and now he knows it. But it's too late.

* * *

Genesis 3 has proved to be nothing short of a major disaster for Adam and Eve in terms of their manhood and womanhood. What began as an excellent relationship in Genesis 1 and 2—two image-bearers who perfectly completed each other—has become totally corrupted and devastated by the end of chapter 3. We are left with the critical question, Is there any hope? We ask because far too many relationships and marriages today are stuck in Genesis 3. Is there any hope? There is a hint at hope; the woman's offspring will eventually crush the serpent's skull according to Genesis 3:15. The hope is fulfilled in the New Testament through a relationship with Christ. We will explore this in part 3.

DISCUSSION QUESTIONS

1. Do you sense as you read Genesis 3:14-15 that God is speaking with someone other than a mere snake? If so, what leads you to think this? Does the New Testament suggest another identity for the serpent (see Rev. 12:9; 20:2)? What are your feelings toward this creature at this point in the story? Why?

2. Have you ever seen a snake crawling across the ground? If you have, what did you think? Now that you are aware of God's curse on the serpent, what will you think of if you should ever see a crawling serpent? Will it remind you of something?

3. The story in Genesis 3:15 is about the conflict between the two seeds. This is *our* story in that the conflict between the two seeds involves the Cross. When Christ died on the cross, he provided the basis for the redemption of you and me. He died to pay for our sins. This in turn provides the basis for the redemption of our relationship with God and our spouse. Have you accepted Christ's payment for your sins? If no, why not? Without accepting Christ, you will never have a proper relationship with God or the opposite sex.

For Women

4. What has caused you the most physical pain in your life? Have you had a child? If yes, how would childbearing compare to any other physical pain you've experienced? According to Genesis 3, what should the pain of childbirth remind you of? Do you believe that sin has its consequences? If you have children, how might you experience emotional pain in bearing or raising them?

5. If you're not married, do you find that there are times in your relationships with men that you, like Carol, want to take control of your situation? Why? If you are married, do you find that often you want to control your husband or have your own way? Why? Are there also times when because of his neglect or

passivity, you have to step in and do for him what he should be doing as the responsible head of the relationship?

6. When you assert your control in your relationship with men, especially a husband, how do they respond? Do they tend to resist you? If so, how? Can some responses be resistance in disguise?

For Men

7. According to Genesis 3:17, is it wrong for you to listen to a woman, such as your wife? What was wrong with Adam's listening to the woman in Genesis 3:1–5? When should you listen and when shouldn't you listen? Have there been times in your relationship when you were listening and you should have been leading? Explain.

8. Have you ever directly disobeyed a clear command from God as Adam did in Genesis 3? What were the circumstances? Were there any consequences? If so, how has this affected your life?

9. Have you ever known what it's like to eke out a living? If yes, explain the circumstances. What did you learn from that situation? Have you ever had a job you didn't enjoy? Why didn't you like it?

10. Have you ever failed in a job situation? How did it make you feel? Does your work give you a sense of competence? Has there ever been a time when you questioned your competence? Do you ever fear that you might fail at something such as your job? How does the fear of failure affect your choice of employment, hobbies, sports, as well as other areas?

Notes

1. Allen P. Ross, *Creation & Blessing: A Guide to the Study and Exposition of Genesis* (Grand Rapids: Baker Book House, 1988), pp. 144–45.

2. John H. Sailhammer, *The Pentatech as Narrative* (Grand Rapids: Zondervan Publishing Company, 1992), p. 106.

3. Many of us are indebted to Susan Foh for her work on this term and the

similarity of the wording between Genesis 4:7 and 3:16. See Susan T. Foh, "What Is the Woman's Desire?" *Westminster Theological Journal* 37 (spring 1975): 380–81. Also, see Ronald B. Allen, *The Majesty of Man* (Portland, Ore.: Multnomah Press, 1984), pp. 145–47.

4. Ross, *Creation & Blessing*, p. 146.

5. Ibid., p. 147.

PART III

The Redemption
of Human Sexuality

When we left Adam and Eve in Genesis 3, their relationship had turned ugly. Yet their world is our world—the real world—as we have come to know it. Is there any hope? The curse and judgment on Satan in Genesis 3:15 provide us with a gleam of hope. There was the hint that a future seed, Christ, would crush Satan's head. This was the promise of redemption for mankind through Christ. Not only would Christ make possible the redemption of our relationship with God, but the relationship between a man and a woman. This is realized and proclaimed in the New Testament. Chapter 6 will present the redemptive role of a woman, and chapter 7 will present that of the man from the New Testament.

6

The Redemptive Role of the Woman

The Fine Art of Submission

I t had been a long, difficult month since Randy and Carol Brown had returned from their vacation in Hawaii. They had enjoyed their getaway to Honolulu so much, but no sooner had they landed in Dallas when they were greeted with July summer temperatures that fluctuated between the high 90s and low 100s. The humidity hovered around 80 percent due to an unusually wet and stormy spring and a tropical disturbance situated near the lower coast of western Mexico. The winds that regularly blew from the southeast to the northwest across Mexico during the stifling summer months brought the humidity to Dallas as well as to the rest of Texas, providing a natural sauna-like experience whether the residents appreciated it or not.

Regardless, Carol and Randy felt refreshed emotionally. They didn't realize how much stress they had accumulated over the last two years, from their marriage as well as from their work and ministry at the church. They returned with smiles on their faces, a better outlook on life, and relatively stress free. There is something about getting away from it all and being near the beach that relaxes a person. Perhaps it's the sound of the ocean coupled with a lack of deadlines and the absence of a telephone that works miracles for so many vacationers. The vacation had also affected their appearance. Randy's skin was in the final stages of peeling while Carol's olive complexion hadn't changed all that much.

Most important for them as a couple, they were now able to talk more and reconnect as a man and woman. Randy, like most men, was

115

ready to resume their conversation right where they had left it the last time they intensely interacted over their marriage. She, like most women, needed some time—in this case a day or two—to warm up to the topic. There were several accusations and a few tears, balanced with many hugs and kisses and some time for careful reflection. They began their conversations convinced that the other person was to blame for their difficulties, but ended realizing that "it takes two to tango." Both concluded that while the problem was theirs, it was bigger than both of them and they would need some outside help in working through some of the issues.

Randy had decided to turn to Fellowship Community Church for their counsel and advice. The church had recently added another counselor, Steve Smith, to their staff, and he felt that he could help Carol and Randy. Steve had a master's degree in counseling and was completing a doctorate with a specialty in marriage and family counseling. He also had a seminary degree from an evangelical school. Steve based much of his counseling on the Scriptures, and he was eager to invest in Randy's and Carol's lives as a man and woman. What was to follow would have a profound impact on their marriage and would save them much needless pain over their ensuing years together. Later, when they reflected on their time with Steve, they were convinced that it wasn't any psychological techniques that he used, but it was his understanding of, and insight into, the Scriptures that made such a significant difference in their relationship. In particular, he had developed a biblical view of womanhood and manhood that helped them to understand and relate to one another as God intended.

What had Carol learned about herself and her womanhood that would make a difference in her marriage and relationship with Randy? What does it mean to be an authentic Christian woman? Steve's approach was to explore and help her come to an understanding of her redemptive role as a woman in Christ. Then Steve coached her in the application of this truth to her marriage. They began with the primary problem—Carol's take-charge approach to their relationship—and then, in time, they moved to a redemptive solution— her need to be a submissive helper to her husband.

THE PRIMARY PROBLEM FOR THE WOMAN

Randy had already uncovered the primary problem with Carol from his perspective. On several occasions, he expressed his deep concern that she was trying to change and improve him. She hadn't overtly taken over their relationship, but at times she was very critical of him and offered a lot of unsolicited advice. Whenever he made a mistake, she was right on cue with, "I told you so!" She could also be very demanding. He was convinced that she didn't have a lot of confidence in him and his abilities as a husband, and this had begun to eat away at him.

We discovered in the last chapter that Randy's concern regarding his manhood is valid. In Genesis 3 God judged the man and woman for their disobedience. Ross observes a vital point regarding the judgments in Genesis 3: "They are not commandments to be obeyed but declarations of how life must now be."[1] God's judgment on Eve in Genesis 3:16 affected her to the very core of her sexuality. Not only would she and all women experience pain in childbearing, but they would be predisposed to attempt to master the man. That's the problem and that's how life would now be for the woman in relation to the man.

A Sense of Vulnerability

The cause for her problem of needing to control essentially is the judgment on the woman. She will struggle with her inward desire to take over in her relationship with a man. This desire will not change; it's how life must now be. There's a factor, though, that was present before the judgment and that is also a part of woman's predisposition. It's her heightened sense of vulnerability. How does a woman's vulnerability contribute to problems in the marital relationship?

In Genesis 3:1–5, when Satan tempted Eve, he essentially exploited her vulnerability as a woman and took advantage of her role as a primary helper.

God had designated Eve to function as a helper in her relationship with Adam. Satan, in all his subtlety (Gen. 3:1), however, used her to help him in his attempts to cause a cosmic coup. This took place at a time in her life when she was oblivious to evil and most vulnerable (Gen. 2:25). She and Adam were intimate in the garden. They spent time in conversation and were able to share their inner feelings and empathize with one another. She was open, fully trusting, and thus very vulnerable. Trust was all she had ever known in her brief time on planet earth. She had no idea that this serpent would exploit her vulnerability in his efforts to sabotage God's plan.

In her primary role today as a helper and responder
in a fallen world, a woman experiences a
sense of vulnerability.

Consequently, in her primary role today as a helper and responder in a fallen world, a woman experiences a sense of vulnerability. It's hidden in her unconscious due to what happened to her great-grandmother Eve. Subconsciously she questions: My great-grandmother Eve was exploited in her vulnerability, will I be? She desperately needs other people in her life, but this makes her vulnerable. So she asks: Can I risk vulnerability? Will I be hurt? Or in many cases, Will I be hurt again? If as a child she witnessed abuse or was directly abused herself, she may find herself even more vulnerable to feelings of helplessness, unworthiness, and shame. Regardless, it becomes difficult for her to determine her worth as a woman, and she needs the love and comfort of her husband. At the same time, however, she fears that he won't be there for her.

A Fear of Desertion

A woman's fear in a significant relationship with a man is desertion. This comes with her heightened sense of vulnerability. She legitimately wants and needs him as he needs her. But she asks: What if I'm not supported? What if I'm abandoned? Or, What if I'm abandoned again? After all, Adam abandoned Eve! Where was Adam when she needed him the most? Adam didn't support Eve emotionally. Most likely he was standing right beside her (Gen. 3:6); however, he wasn't there for her. In short, he deserted her.

Abandonment is very painful for a woman. It sends a message that she's on her own. She feels that a man doesn't care enough to help her or to support or protect her. This is very hard on her self-esteem. If she felt abandoned or rejected by her father, or if her mother felt rejected by her husband, a woman will be even more sensitive to feelings of desertion. Unfortunately, both of these situations are true for many women today, as illustrated in Carol's family. As the divorce rate in America hovers around 50 percent, it is apparent many men have chosen to literally abandon their wives and children. Thus a large number of households are headed by single women. Also, a father may be physically present in a home but absent emotionally.

The problem in many relationships is the man's desire to be seen as competent. The judgment on the man in Genesis 3 was that he would struggle with his competence as a man in what became a somewhat hostile world. Whereas before the Fall, the world melted with Adam's touch, after the Fall it became rebellious and resistant to his efforts to rule it. This results in much stress and is very hard on the male ego. It's a manhood issue. When he begins to question his competence, he feels a deep impact on his confidence. Consequently, in today's stressful world, men need time to themselves to wrestle with these issues. Therefore, they tend to withdraw from their relationships for what are usually short periods of time to work on their problems in pursuit of a sense or feeling of competence.

Desertion is a woman's fear in a significant relationship with a man. She asks, What if I'm not supported? What if I'm abandoned?

What women don't realize is that these men will reach a point when they'll come back to them. You'll recall that in Genesis 2:18 God created the man with a gaping void in his life. He was relationally incomplete, resulting in an intense relational loneliness. Once he solves a few problems and begins to feel competent again, he suddenly becomes acutely aware of his loneliness as a man. He senses that someone very important is missing from his life. He misses his connectedness with a woman and senses that he's not complete. So he'll return to the woman in his life. His absence may be a matter of only a few hours or as much as a few days. Withdrawal is natural to a man and women should expect it. The solution is for her to be patient. It's crucial that when he returns that he not be greeted with hostility or antagonism, but with understanding. Otherwise, her hostility could lead to emotional and physical desertion.

There are other times when men wrongfully desert women. Often this takes place when a woman needs him the most such as when she is feeling upset, confused, displeased, or overwhelmed. At these times women need to sense that they aren't alone. The men in their lives don't recognize what is taking place. They don't understand a woman's feelings and often assume that much of her displeasure is directed at them when it's not. Also, men simply don't know what to do or how to respond when a woman is needy, which only heightens their feelings of incompetence. So men become frightened or indifferent and distance themselves emotionally. Women interpret the man's withdrawal as abandonment, and they feel ignored, deserted, and hurt. They assume that men are rejecting them and become resentful, which only makes the situation worse.

Discomfort with Her Womanhood

The result of all this for a woman is that she becomes very uncomfortable with her sexuality, her womanhood. In particular, she's distressed with her function as a primary helper. She may grow resentful and distance him or become afraid and run after him. Eve failed to be a helper both during the temptation and when she shifted all the blame for her actions to the serpent. Rather than assuming the guilt for what she'd done, she played the "blame game" or, more accurately, the "shift the blame game"—the serpent made me do it!

The result for a woman is that she becomes very uncomfortable with her womanhood.

Now it will be difficult to function as a helper and responder to a man. It's not easy to give a man some room because it feels like he's abandoning her. She wonders if she's done something wrong that's turned him off. If she asks, most likely he won't be able to give her a clear answer. He's not sure that he understands himself. She may even wrongly assume that he doesn't love her. In addition, how does she know for sure that he'll come back, or if he'll come back this time? What if he doesn't? This anxiety is anything but pleasant. Consequently, she'll tend to resist his withdrawal and resort to various devices in an attempt to change him. Some woman will even go so far as to deny their role and embrace a hard-core feminist approach to manhood-womanhood issues.

The Woman's Solution

Her solution to his withdrawal is to do what comes naturally. She'll attempt to control the man in her life (Gen. 3:16). This is natural for her since the Fall. This is the way life will be because of Eve's sin and the ensuing judgment. A woman feels most powerful and comfortable with being in control of her relationships, especially with a man. In control she finds safety and security. Control takes a variety of forms ranging from being demanding on the one extreme to being a doormat on the other (fig. 1).

FORMS OF CONTROL
Demanding—Criticizing—Quarreling—Advising—Silence—Super Sweet—Doormat

(Figure 1)

Demanding. One form of control is being demanding. In Genesis 30:1, Rachel realized that she was infertile. At the same time, she also became jealous of her sister who was fertile. The hurt she experienced over her infertility combined with her jealousy resulted in her demanding a child from Jacob: "Give me children, or I'll die!"

Rachel didn't blame her husband, but she saw him as a potential solution to her problem—he could give her a child through her servant Bilhah (v. 4). Jacob misunderstood and interpreted her demand as blaming him for her condition. Consequently, he became very angry with her: "Am I in the place of God, who has kept you from having children?" (v. 3). When women complain about a situation or make demands of their husbands, men typically assume that women are blaming them.

While a woman such as Rachel may get her way (Bilhah provided her with a son), she will often incur the wrath of her husband in the process. She's unknowingly challenged his manhood. At some point she must ask: Is it worth it? In the long term, being demanding is very harmful and will seriously damage their relationship.

Criticizing. Often a woman will attempt to get her way through criticizing the man. This is her way of telling him what to do. She may criticize what he does for a living. For example, he may be an excellent bookkeeper, but she'll complain that he should have been a CPA. She might criticize how well he accomplishes his work. He may be good at what he does, but she always finds fault with it. Some women also criticize their man's appearance. They don't like the way the man dresses or brushes his hair, so they criticize in hopes that he'll respond and change. Some women criticize how their husbands provide for them because they desire a better lifestyle. They want men to provide the kind of income that would allow them to live at a higher social level.

The problem is that criticism makes him feel less of a man. Whether or not she realizes it, she is sending him the message that he's inadequate and the implication only damages the male ego. He feels unloved, unacceptable, and taken for granted. Though wrong, his response to her will be negative. Whatever she wants, he'll be sure to resist it. Resistance is a poor reaction on his part that only further complicates matters, and the relationship further deteriorates.

Quarreling. Another form of control is quarreling and nagging. Proverbs 27:15 says: "A quarrelsome wife is like a constant dripping on a rainy day; restraining her is like restraining the wind or grasping oil with the hand." Alden writes: "Here she is likened to the monotonous 'dripping on a rainy day.' No one is able to stop her from complaining. Restraining her is as futile as 'stopping the wind' or 'trying to hold oil in your hand.'"[2]

The point is that this kind of woman is unpleasant to everyone. No one appreciates her or enjoys being around her, especially her husband. Most men respond to this kind of control by distancing themselves from her. While she may get what she wants, she loses relationally in the long term.

Advising. A fourth form of control is unsolicited advice. Women are often prone to give men advice. When a man is struggling with his competence and working on his problems, she may innocently try to help him solve some of those problems. After all, that's how women help one another. It's important to him, though, to solve those problems on his own. If she solves them, then that proves *her* competence, not his, and might serve to make him look bad. He prefers to solve his problems alone. That's why her advice is not solicited. Most men tend not to ask women for advice, especially when they feel incompetent because they sense the need to prove their own competence.

When she offers advice, he also feels as if she doesn't really trust him and his abilities. In short, he may already be struggling with feelings of incompetence from his work or some other activity. When she gives him advice or makes a suggestion, he interprets this as her questioning his competence. This serves only to frustrate him and compound his problem.

Silence. A fifth form of control is silence. Some women attempt to control their husbands through giving them the "silent treatment." This serves as a continual irritating reminder that there's something wrong with their relationship that is his fault and needs to be fixed. Yet she'll quietly distance him and resist his natural but futile attempts to fix it.

Not only does the man sense her disapproval, but he feels a growing resentment toward her. Her silence doesn't bring him around or cause him to apologize for anything he may have said or done. It simply makes him even more angry with her. He can get by without her emotional support or presence better than she can get by without his. She needs it more than he does. Consequently, the situation becomes worse. Most often his response is to clam up and wait her out. He knows from experience that in time she'll give in first. As she attempts to control him, he dominates her (Gen. 3:16).

Super Sweet. Some women attempt to influence men by being super sweet. This may characterize women who are always giving much in their relationships. They're convinced that their role in life is to be sweet and cordial, and that's okay if they are doing this in service of the Savior. For some women, however, there is an ulterior motive— they expect much in return.

This form of control always surprises people; they think that it's the other way around, that the man is controlling the woman. But some women have discovered that by being super sweet they ultimately get their way. Super sweetness is another form of manipulation and control. The problem is that over time a woman may build up a resentment toward others because she has given more than she'll ever get in return.

The Doormat. Another form of self-protective control is the doormat. This is the woman who lets other people, especially men, walk all over her. Chances are that people have walked all over her throughout her life. This began early, often with a dominant father, and the woman has come to accept it as a way of life. If she is a Christian, she may assume that being submissive means letting people abuse her emotionally and possibly physically, depending on what has taken place in her childhood. Some women relate to men this way because they have discovered that, like super sweet women, they can get their way with their husbands. They pay a tremendous price emotionally, but they ultimately get what they want as well as find safety and pain relief in this role.

THE TRAGEDY

The tragedy is that all of this is very destructive! In spite of all the energy expended, neither the man nor the woman gets what they want or what is best for either of them. Most often the result is much hurt, deep resentment, and the eventual unraveling of the relationship.

It Never Works for the Woman

When a woman seeks to control a man so that he'll meet her deepest needs, it's like taking baby aspirin to cure terminal cancer. Attempting to control a man simply doesn't work for several reasons. First, the woman is not properly relating to him. She's not functioning in her natural, God-given role as a primary, supportive helper. Like Eve, she's usurped his role in their relationship. She doesn't complete him in the way God designed. Consequently, although she'll experience some temporary pain relief, she'll never be really satisfied with the relationship nor her role in it.

It's as if she's taking baby aspirin as a sure cure
for terminal cancer.

Second, she's suffocated as a woman, or more accurately self-suffocated. Because she's not properly relating to her husband, she's functioning contrary to God's design for her. Consequently, she'll not know the fulfillment that God has in store for her when she's rightly relating to her husband. While sin has deeply scarred their relationship, every Christian man and woman can experience, to some degree, the intimacy that Adam and Eve experienced in the garden in Genesis 2:25. They can only realize authentic intimacy, however, when both embrace their God-designed roles in the relationship.

Third, the woman's controlling behavior is self-defeating. Her desire is for deep intimacy. Instead, she's pushing him away, and, tragically, she doesn't even realize it. He senses her disrespect (Eph. 5:33) and resents it. She is aiding and abetting what she fears the most—his abandoning her. Women need to understand that when they demand, criticize, give advice, and so on that men feel controlled, unloved, and unsupported. They believe that their competence is being questioned whether that's true or not. Their natural response is to resist women's efforts and to distance them emotionally and even physically.

It Never Works for the Man

Genesis 3:16 indicates that the man will respond to the woman's compulsive desire to control him by dominating her in one way or another. He may actively or passively resist her efforts. When he doesn't feel unconditionally loved, he will either consciously or unconsciously repeat the behavior she so strongly resists. He's stubborn and will often repeat the same behavior until he feels unconditionally accepted by her.

When a man believes that a woman is trying to control or change him through some of the devices mentioned above, he experiences various negative feelings. Her repeated advice, no matter how harmless, may leave him feeling unloved and untrusted. He feels that she doesn't accept him unconditionally. Her complaints about what he hasn't done make him feel unappreciated for all that he has done for her. He wants to be the object of her admiration, her knight in shining armor, but he feels the opposite when she criticizes or corrects him (especially in public) or attempts to tell him what to do. She becomes a constant irritant and a source of intense pain for him. Consequently, like a man who has touched a hot pan on a kitchen stove, his natural response is to pull away from her to relieve his pain.

When a woman seeks to influence or change a man, he feels that she's questioning his competence as a man.

The primary, overarching problem is a man's feelings of incompetence. That's his judgment, however, that's the way life will be for him since the Fall (Gen. 3:17–19). Thus, when a woman seeks to change a man, she's questioning his very competence. When this happens repeatedly, he is convinced that she views him as a failure. This leaves him with a growing sense of impotence that robs him of any desire to meet her deep felt needs. He grows to deeply resent her, and he builds huge walls of resistance to her efforts to change him. This leads to male dominance that has the potential to get very ugly.

THE REDEMPTIVE SOLUTION FOR THE WOMAN

In Genesis 2:18, we discovered that God designed the woman to be a primary, supportive helper in her complementary relationship with a man. But because of the Fall she'll attempt to control or take over her husband, resulting in his dominance of her (Gen. 3:16). That's how life will be for her from now on here on planet earth.

The question is, Can anything be done about her situation? What has Christ done that could help her in her relationship with a man? What difference can Christ make in her relationship? The answer is found in the New Testament. The solution to her problem is a redemptive relationship that is based on the Cross of Christ as predicted in Genesis 3:15. Because of his great love, the Redeemer, Jesus Christ, models what it means for a man to live in relationship with a woman. As the church follows Christ, His redeemed community, it models what it means for a woman to live in relationship with her husband (Eph. 5:24). This chapter emphasizes the latter.

The redemptive role for the woman is to be a
submissive helper to her husband.

Every passage in the New Testament that addresses the wife's relationship with her husband directs her to submit to him (Eph. 5:22, Col. 3:18, 1 Peter 3:1–6, and Titus 2:5). The New Testament strongly emphasizes a wife's submission in following her husband's leadership. Therefore, the redemptive role for the woman is to be a submissive helper to her husband. But this is a strong term that today's women may find offensive. Thus the word submission raises several questions: What does this mean? How is she to submit? and, Why should she submit to him? In Ephesians 5:22 Paul answers these questions as he presents the what, how, and why of biblical submission for the woman.

The Wife Is to Submit to Her Husband

In Epehsians 5:21 Paul encourages Christians to mutual submission as members of the body of Christ: "Submit to one another out of reverence for Christ." This is the same kind of exhortation as Philippians 2:3–4: "Do nothing out of selfish ambition or vain conceit, but in humility consider others better than yourselves. Each of you should look not only to your own interests, but also to the interests of others." This serves as his introduction to Ephesians 5:22–6:9 where Paul spells out how various groups—wives and husbands, children and parents, even slaves and masters—should exhibit submission in their particular relationships.

Though the wife is equal to her husband, as they function together in a team, she is to be submissive to him as the responsible leader of the team.

In verse 22 Paul commands: "Wives, submit to your husbands. . . ." In chapter 2, we discovered that the primary role of Eve and all women is that of an equal helper (Gen. 2:18). While outside the context of Scripture this might seem rather cold and demeaning to some women, actually it's not. The term "helper" was also used of God (Exod. 18:4; Deut. 33:7; 1 Sam. 7:12, and other passages). A woman was, and is, a "helper" in the sense that she completes the man; she brings to their relationship that which he can't supply. He needs her and she needs him; together they wonderfully complete one another. We also discovered that a subset of the woman's function as a helper was to follow, respond, receive, support, and so on. Here in Ephesians 5, Paul adds to the subset the responsibility to submit. That every reference dealing with the wife-husband relationship in the New Testament includes the wife's submission is significant. It's a most important concept in the life of a man and a woman and their relationship together in Christ. The clear emphasis from the New Testament is that a wife such as Carol is to be not only a helper to her husband, but a submissive helper. Though she is equal to her husband (Gen. 1), as they function together in a team, she is to be submissive to him as the responsible leader of their team.

The question is, What does it mean for a wife to submit to her husband? Specifically, What does it mean for Carol to submit to Randy? Submission has become a problematic concept for so many Christian women in twentieth-century America. On the one hand, they recognize that submission is a valid, biblical term; on the other hand, it can sound so harsh to the female ear. I'm convinced that this is the result of its sinful abuse, not its proper use. Therefore, an explanation is imperative.

Sometimes it helps to understand a concept first by looking at what it doesn't mean. The wife's submission to her husband doesn't mean that she is a doormat. We've already discussed this to some extent earlier in this chapter. When a man walks all over a woman, it's abuse. It may involve emotional abuse where he treats her as an unequal, inferior person. He may attempt to restrict and control her friendships and activities outside the home, and he may not trust her with the finances even when she might be the primary breadwinner. It could also include such things as his trying to fix her rather than listening to her when she comes to him with her problems. It may involve physical abuse whereby he hits his wife. Abuse is most demeaning to women and is a by-product of the male domination that came as the result of the Fall (Gen. 3:16). Male domination is a complete violation of the equality of women and men as created in God's image (Gen. 1) and undermines a couple's oneness in Christ (Gal. 3:28).

> *Submission means that a wife isn't to attempt to control her husband.*

Biblical submission is not a dominant-passive relationship between a husband and his wife. Yet some mistakenly think that submissive women are to be passive women. They believe that a wife should not think for herself or tell her husband how she feels about an issue, and she's to meet his every demand without question. Nowhere does Scripture condone this thought or behavior. Instead, biblical examples such as the Proverbs 31 woman (who is anything but passive) clearly contradict this.

Now that we have an understanding of what submission isn't, what does it entail? What does Paul mean when he directs a wife to submit to her husband? Is this merely the chauvinist ranting of a frustrated bachelor? There are several good answers to this critical relational question. We'll examine two.

First, it means that she's not to attempt to control her husband. Paul knew and understood well Genesis 1–3. In several passages in the New Testament that address the relationship between men and women and husbands and wives, he refers to these chapters as a basis for some vital relational principle. For example, in 1 Corinthians 11:8–10 he refers to the woman's creation from and for the man in Genesis 2 to establish the principle that a woman is to honor her husband. In 1 Timothy 2:11–14 he refers to Genesis 2–3 in establishing the woman's role in the church.

> *Submission means that the woman recognizes*
> *and honors the authority of her husband*
> *to lead in their marriage.*

I believe that Paul is doing the same thing in Ephesians 5:22. Genesis 1–3 forms the backdrop for Ephesians 5:22–33. He even quotes from Genesis 2:24 in verse 31. He is aware of the judgment in Genesis 3:16 and the resulting temptation for a woman to want to control her relationship with a man. Consequently, Paul responds and says to wives, don't attempt to control your husbands. Instead, put the shoe on the other foot—you don't appreciate your husband's attempts to control you, why are you attempting to control them?

Randy's complaints about Carol's tendencies to dominate him are probably true in light of Genesis 3:16. Thus Paul is saying to Carol whenever she feels tempted to take control in their relationship, she must not. The only person she can control is herself, not Randy. Carol must work hard at resisting the temptation to control Randy even when she believes that he is wrong. What Carol, and all women, must realize is that to control a man is to demean his sense of competence, whereas to resist the temptation increases his feeling of competence. A woman's loving submission to her husband is the secret to empowering him to address her deepest, most significant needs.

Second, submission means that the woman recognizes and honors her husband's authority to lead in their marriage. The New Testament uses the term "authority" in a number of passages as placing oneself under the authority of another. In Romans 13 Paul used it in terms of the Christian's responsibility to be under the authority of the civil government. In Hebrews 12 and James 4 the writers used it in terms of putting oneself under the authority of God. In Hebrews 13 the writer used it in terms of placing oneself under the authority of the elders (the equivalent of today's pastor) of the church. In Ephesians 5 and Colossians 3 there's no reason to think that Paul is using the term any differently. He's urging wives to place themselves under the authority of their husbands. Since God holds the husband responsible for their relationship, he gives the husband authority commensurate with that responsibility. I'll say more about this below.

The Wife Is to Submit to Her Husband as to Christ

Paul further instructs wives in Ephesians 5:22 to submit to their husbands "as to the Lord." Here we discover how a woman is to submit to a man. She is to submit to her husband as she would submit to Christ. This helps to further clarify the meaning of submission. When a woman submits to Christ, he would never use her as a doormat. The idea that the loving Savior would emotionally or physically abuse a woman is repugnant. The same applies to the dominant-passive approach to female submission. When a woman submits to Christ, that doesn't mean that she suddenly becomes passive in the relationship or that she can no longer show any initiative or think for herself.

> *When a woman submits to Christ, that doesn't mean that she suddenly becomes passive in the relationship or that she can no longer show any initiative or think for herself.*

When a woman submits to a man, however, she places herself in a vulnerable situation in which he could take advantage of her. Most women know and sense their vulnerability, and this, along with numerous negative examples of abuse, explains why the biblical term "submission" is so negative to many women. Regardless, a woman must realize that God has only her best interests at heart. He would not ask her to do anything that would harm her or expose her to any form of abuse. But to submit to a man sounds so risky! It certainly makes a woman vulnerable to an abusive situation, which is one of the reasons why she wants to gain control in the first place. Nevertheless, Christ is saying through Paul that the wife is to take the risk. And that if she has been abused in another relationship with a father or former husband, in the new relationship she's to take the risk again.

But what are some practical ways that a wife can submit to her husband? What does biblical submission look like in Carol's relationship with Randy? Here are a few suggestions. First, she is submissive when she doesn't tell him what to do. For example, she might request that he let the dog out, rather than tell him or demand it. He may be planning already to let the dog out, or he may be putting it off for a good or a bad reason. Regardless, when you tell him to let the dog out, especially in a demanding tone, he interprets this as control and will resist. He will either drag his heels, or he may never let the dog out, much to the detriment of the animal.

Second, she is submissive when she asks for his help in the right way. When she requests that he do something for her it's very important that she use the terms "would" or "will" and not "could" or "can." Not only is it grammatically correct, but it is relationally correct. If she asks, "Can you let the dog out" or "could you let the dog out?" unless he's physically disabled or incapacitated in some way the answer is yes. To a man the question that uses could or can negatively challenges his competence. Who can't let the dog out?

It's better for a woman to ask, Would or will you let the dog out? This positively communicates her confidence that he has the competence to pull it off as well as any other request. When she asks using "could" or "can," she turns him off, and he may not respond at all. But if she asks using "would" or "will," he's turned on, and he'll climb the nearest mountain for her. She sends him the important message that she believes in him and his ability to do things for her.

Third, she is submissive when she shows appreciation for what he does for her. Both men and women often fail to show appreciation for one another's contributions to the relationship. But the focus here is on a wife showing appreciation to her husband. When she consistently fails to do this, the husband feels taken for granted and will not respond well to her needs or requests. Whereas when she shows appreciation, he feels valued and respected for his capabilities, and he'll want to do things for her. This affirms his competence—it's a male thing.

These suggestions and others are labeled submissive because they are not controlling or manipulative in action or intent. They recognize and honor a man, and, most importantly, they convey that his wife believes in him and believes that he's competent as a man. In light of the Fall and the judgment on the man, he needs to hear from someone who's very important and close, someone who knows him best, that he's a winner.

The Wife Is to Submit to Her Husband Because He Is the Responsible Leader

Ephesians 5:23 provides the reason the wife is to submit to her husband: "For the husband is the head of the wife as Christ is the head of the church, his body, of which he is the Savior." Paul is saying that a woman is to submit to her husband because God has made him the responsible, serving head of their relationship.

This is a reference to the headship of the husband in the divine-human hierarchy. According to passages such as 1 Corinthians 11:3; 3:23; and 15:23, God has set up a divine-human hierarchy. First Corinthians 11:3 is the key verse. Paul writes: "Now I want you to realize that the head of every man is Christ, and the head of the woman is man, and the head of Christ is God." Figure 2 displays this hierarchy.

THE DIVINE–HUMAN HIERARCHY

(Figure 2)

This hierarchy is not based in any way on a person's value or worth. Just as Christ and the Father are equal, so are the man and the woman (in context a husband and wife). What this hierarchy represents is a line of authority or responsibility. God is the responsible party and point person in the Trinity, and the man is the same in the husband-wife relationship. The husband has the authority; therefore, he also has the responsibility that accompanies that authority. If something goes wrong in a family, God looks to the husband first, not the wife, as the responsible agent. Should something go wrong in Carol's and Randy's marriage, God will look to Randy first as the responsible party. It's most important to their marriage that Carol recognize and honor this.

Consequently, as Christ models submission to the Father as the responsible lead person in the Trinity, so the wife models submission to the husband as the responsible lead person in their marriage. Thus, a woman is most like Christ in her marriage when she willingly, lovingly submits to the leadership of her husband.

A woman is most like Christ in her marriage when she willingly, lovingly submits to the leadership of her husband.

But what about the woman who finds herself in a marriage with a non-Christian or a disobedient Christian? The discussion in this chapter has assumed that the husband is walking with Christ and has his wife's best interests at heart. This may not be the case. Does a woman have to submit to an unbelieving or disobedient husband? In 1 Peter 3:1–2, Peter writes: "Wives, in the same way be submissive to your husbands so that, if any of them do not believe the word, they may be won over without words by the behavior of their wives, when they see the purity and reverence of your lives."

Peter explains that it doesn't matter if the husband is a believer or unbeliever, carnal or spiritual, the wife is to submit to his leadership. The judgment in Genesis 3:16 affects all marriages regardless of the spiritual condition of the man or woman. Unbelieving and carnal Christian men don't want a controlling wife any more than a spiritual Christian man. The point is that a woman's loving submission may contribute to either the husband's salvation or to a return to Christ.

DISCUSSION QUESTIONS

For Women

1. Do you as a woman ever struggle with vulnerability? If yes, explain. In your relationships with men, do you feel a sense of vulnerability? Do you ever ask, Will I be hurt in this relationship, or will I be hurt again? If yes, why do you feel this way?

2. In a significant relationship with a man, do you ever fear that he might desert or abandon you? Explain. Has a man such as your father, boyfriend, or husband ever deserted you emotionally or physically? If you've been abandoned, how did you feel about yourself?

3. Have you noticed that men have a pattern of going away and then coming back in their relationships with women? Has this happened to you? How do you feel about this pattern? How might you explain it? What do you do when it happens to you? What should you do when it happens to you?

4. Deep within do you feel a compulsion to take control in your relationships with men (boyfriend, husband, and so on)? In what ways do you attempt to control men? Does it work? Does it ever work? How does this affect you? How does it affect him?

5. The term "submission" is biblical. Do you react positively or negatively to it? How would you explain your reaction? Do you feel good about the command in Ephesians 5:22 for the wife to submit to her husband? Why or why not? What does it mean for a woman to submit to her husband? What doesn't it mean?

6. If you're a wife, do you submit to your husband? Why or why not? If or when you do, what does it look like? Do you feel vulnerable? If yes, why? Are you vulnerable? If yes, what should you do about it?

7. Why should a wife submit to her husband? What does Paul mean when he says that the husband is head over the wife? If you're married, is your husband an unbeliever or carnal Christian? If yes, should you submit to his leadership? Why? Will you submit to his leadership?

Notes

1. Allen P. Ross, *Creation & Blessing: A Guide to the Study and Exposition of Genesis* (Grand Rapids: Baker Book House, 1988), p. 144.

2. Robert L. Alden, *Proverbs: A Commentary on An Ancient Book of Timeless Advice* (Grand Rapids: Baker Book House, 1983), p. 192.

7

The Redemptive Role of the Man
Loving Leadership

Carol believes that Steve Smith's counsel from the Scriptures, particularly Ephesians 5, has helped her to understand Randy better and what her responsibilities are to him as her husband. But as both will discover, this passage is no magic wand that they can wave over their marriage and instantly make it better. There is no magical formula that will make a marriage work. In spite of what Carol has learned, she will still fail Randy as a wife. But God can use this potential failure to point Carol and Randy to Himself.

Steve's biblical counseling has helped Randy as well as Carol. What has Randy learned about himself and his manhood? What has he learned that has helped his marriage and given him insight into himself as a man? Steve has opened the Scriptures to Randy and helped him to understand his redemptive role and responsibility in his relationship with Carol. As Steve coached Carol, so he coached Randy in the application of this biblical truth to their marriage. First, they wrestled together with the primary problem—Randy's compulsive desire to dominate Carol. Next, they explored the redemptive solution—Randy's need to be the loving leader of their home.

THE PRIMARY PROBLEM FOR THE MAN

Carol has made it clear on several occasions that she was disappointed with Randy's passivity during their two years of marriage. She suspects that now she understands how Eve felt in the Garden when Adam wasn't there for her emotionally. She feels very vulnerable in their relationship. She still remembers the sense of worthlessness and shame she experienced when her father left her and her mother. Initially she assumed that it was her fault. Counseling has helped her a lot with all that baggage.

In her marriage and commitment to Randy, Carol has taken the risk to be vulnerable again, and it was okay for a while. But those feelings have begun to show up again. She feels that he abandons her relationally. Not all the time, but enough to frighten her. Her response has been to take charge in order to protect herself from her disappointment with his lack of care and protection. No one except Randy has made a strong emotional investment in her life, and that was while they were dating and early in their marriage. Now he seems to pull back, and many of her longings have gone unrealized. Therefore, at various times she has tried to contol Randy in a desperate attempt to get him to meet her needs and to try to silence those painful feelings from her past.

In Genesis 3 God says that Adam's response to the woman's attempts to take him over will be to rule or dominate her.

What is the problem? In Genesis 3 God says that Adam's response to the woman's attempts to control him will be to rule or dominate her (Gen. 3:16). This is the way life will be not only for Adam and Eve, but for all men and women. The woman will be predisposed to control the man, and he will respond by dominating her. Randy's passive behavior appears to be anything but dominating, but it is as we shall see.

A Feeling of Incompetence

The cause for Randy's dominance and that of other men is a profound wrongful sense of incompetence or inadequacy as a man. This was the result of God's judgment on Adam in Genesis 3:17–19. In Genesis 3:17 God cursed the ground as the result of Adam's sin. Adam isn't a victim in all this, it's what he deserved. He brought it all on himself. Regardless, this meant that it would no longer be easy to rule the world. From here on it will tenaciously resist his best efforts. It will feed him but will require painful toil to do so. He will sow good seed only to reap thorns and thistles. He will know frustration and humiliation as never before. This will leave him with a profound sense of inadequacy. Whereas he knew only success, now he'll know what it's like to experience failure. Consequently, a man's deepest fear is incompetence. The last thing he wants to hear is that he's not competent as a man. Deep within his unconscious he already suspects it. All he needs is to mess up to prove that it's true, and there's no question that he'll eventually mess up.

A man's deepest fear is incompetence. The last things he wants to hear is that he's not competent as a man.

A classic example of a failed attempt at leadership is Moses' debacle in Exodus 2–3. He killed an Egyptian in an attempt to show his people that God was going to use him to rescue them from slavery in Egypt (Exod. 2:11–12). But instead of following him, they turned on him (v. 14). Their response was total rejection, and his response was to flee the scene of the crime—to disappear. He had failed miserably in his first attempt as a potential leader. His brash action in killing the Egyptian demonstrated his incompetence.

What kind of impact did this experience have on his confidence and his feelings of competence as a leader? The answer is in Exodus 3. After forty years of tending sheep in the desert, Moses was confronted by God, who appeared to him in a burning bush and announced that it was time for Moses to lead Israel out of Egypt (Exod. 3:1–10). Moses' response in verse 11 demonstrates the fragile nature of the male ego: "Who am I, that I should go to Pharaoh and bring the Israelites out of Egypt?" Forty years had passed, and Moses is still convinced that he's totally incompetent as a leader. His initial failure only confirmed his worst fear—that he really is a loser and he's never recovered. Confidence is the child of competence, but Moses is related to neither. Consequently, God spends the next chapter and a half convincing Moses that he will be with him. The point is that Moses' competence and ensuing confidence would come from God, not himself or his abilities. Later Paul will drive home this message in 2 Corinthians 3:4–6.

A Fear of Failure

God has designed men such as Randy to be the responsible leaders in the families (Gen. 2–3 and 1 Cor. 11). Yet secretly men question their competence to lead. So they ask certain competency questions. A single man who's considering marriage asks: Can I lead this woman? Can I take the primary responsibility for our new relationship? And a married man asks: Am I leading this woman? Have I taken the primary responsibility for our relationship?

At the very heart of the competency question looms the issue of failure. Men are asking: What if I fail?

At the very heart of the competency question looms the issue of failure. Men are also asking: What if I fail? After all, Adam failed twice—he failed both God and Eve at the Temptation (Gen. 3:1–5) and later at under God's interrogation (Gen. 3:11–12). As I said above, a man's greatest fear now is incompetence. Men are afraid that they may fail at what they do. The problem in America, as well as other cultures, is that people (men in particular) measure a man's worth by his accomplishments. This is a major reason why white men over the age of 65 represent the most suicide-prone group in the country. Among people over age 65 who commit suicide, four out of five are white men.[1] Most men from the preboomer era have defined themselves by their work. So when they retire or stop doing what they do, their sense of devaluation is incredible.

Some men will always struggle with a feeling of inadequacy. They're not sure they can do anything well, so they dabble at various jobs for most of their lives. Others will do well in their work and feel good about themselves, then often become driven to be even more successful. But men are so fragile that all it takes is a major failure or a series of minor setbacks, and they begin to seriously doubt themselves. They ask: Can't I cut it anymore? Have I just been lucky in the past? Maybe I really am a loser. The fear of failure and the actual experience of failure can make cowards of us all.

As Randy and Carol have learned, a man's fear of failure especially affects the relationship between him and a woman. Most women don't understand a man's intense fear of failure. Consequently, since no man is perfect, husbands find their wives attempting to change or improve them to meet their unfulfilled expectations. The attempt may involve such devices as a put down, rejection, distancing, blaming, complaining, and so on. But when a woman doesn't like something a man has done and she uses these devices, it says that she doubts his competency as a man and sees him as a failure. This is very painful to a man. He takes it personally and feels that his wife doesn't respect him, and he feels deeply wounded.

This is not to say that a woman must approve of everything a man does. Scripture teaches the principle that when one person sins against another, the offended party is to pursue the offender in hopes of settling the matter (Matt. 5:23–25). The key is how a wife communicates her disapproval. When a man feels accepted, trusted, and appreciated, he's more apt to listen to loving correction. Most wives don't understand this their husband's fear of failure, and thus unknowingly their genuine attempts to help their husbands serve only to damage and further undermine the marriage.

Discomfort with His Manhood

The result of all this fear of failure and incompetency is that the typical man is uncomfortable with his sexuality. It was at the very heart and center of his sexuality that Adam failed. God had made him the responsible leader in their marriage. That was how he would complete Eve. But instead of leading, Adam became passive during Eve's temptation. He was silent and passive when he should have spoken and acted. And later, when God gave Adam a chance to speak and act like a man, to confess his failure and sin, he chose to shift the blame back to his wife and ultimately to God. Thus he failed miserably.

The fact is that being the man that God intended each of them to be puts men in touch with the essence of their failure. Most will profess that accepting the possibility of failure is too painful, and many will avoid their God-given responsibilities.

Adam's failure has become the man's failure. Since the Fall, men have inherited from Adam a natural predisposition not to be there for women when women need them and their leadership, and to shift the blame rather than admit their failures and incompetence. The fact is that being the man that God intended each of them to be puts them in touch with the essence of their failure. Most will profess that accepting the possibility of failure is too painful, and many avoid their God-given responsibilities. To a certain extent, Satan won in the Garden, and unless something changes, he continues to win in the lives of many men today.

The Man's Solution

The man's solution to his problem is to, like the woman, do what comes naturally since the Fall. His fear of incompetence in his relationship with his wife (Gen. 3:17–19) naturally leads to a self-protective dominance that results in some form of abuse (Gen. 3:16). Abusive behavior either makes him feel competent or assuages his feeling of fear and incompetence.

His solution to his problem is . . . to do what comes naturally since the Fall. His fear of incompetence in his relationship with his wife naturally leads to a self-protective dominance that results in some form of abuse.

The man's self-protective dominance can be either active or passive (fig. 1). Active dominance is the extreme perversion of biblical leadership and submission. Under the guise of leadership a man will totally dominate his wife. Men often find themselves in a dominant-passive relationship. One or both individuals view biblical submission as female passivity and strict obedience. She has no mind or opinion of her own. She simply does what he says, no questions asked. Theirs is a president-employee relationship. Like an employee, she has little or no input into the relationship. It's his responsibility to call all the shots.

The parallel passage in the New Testament to Ephesians 5:22–6:9 is Colossians 3:18–4:1. Colossians 3:19 presents the husband's responsibility to his wife: "Husbands, love your wives and do not be harsh with them." As I argued in the last chapter, I believe that Paul is most familiar with Genesis 1–3 and responds to these chapters in such passages as Ephesians 5 and Colossians 3. The last part of Colossians 3:19—"and do not be harsh with them"—is instructive. I believe that here in Colossians 3 Paul is addressing the dominance issue in Genesis 3:16, and active dominance in particular. He's telling men that their responsibility to women is not to exhibit a harsh, active dominance. This is abuse. Love and harshness in a relationship don't mix; they're antithetical. They are not to characterize the marriage of a Christian.

SELF-PROTECTIVE DOMINANCE	
Active Dominance	**Passive Dominance**
Harsh & Overbearing (Gen. 3:16; Col. 3:19)	Weak & Impotent (Gen. 3:1–12)

(Figure 1)

Passive dominance moves to the other extreme. The man in this relationship is weak and impotent. He's like Adam in that he's passive at times in the marriage when he should be active. He's silent when he should be speaking. This is often a dominant-passive relationship, only she's dominant and he's passive. She's dominant by either choice or necessity. Often his lack of leadership creates a vacuum and she moves in and fills it. She reasons: "After all, somebody's got to exercise some leadership around here, somebody's got to make some decisions."

We saw that Colossians 3:19 instructs men not to be harsh with their wives. Instead they are to be proactive with them. They are to take an active part in the leadership of their homes (Gen. 2–3 and 1 Cor. 11). And the New Testament adds in Ephesians 5:25 as well as Colossians 3:19 that husbands are to proactively love their wives.

Somewhere in between harshness and proactivity, and leaning to one extreme or the other, are several things men do that tend to abuse women. One is that they minimize a woman's feelings. Few men seem to understand a woman's feelings and believe that women are far too emotional. Consequently, they respond by playing down those feelings or abandon women during critical situations to fend for themselves. This only serves to leave a woman feeling judged, unsupported, and unimportant.

Another form of abuse that men are hard on women when they

become frustrated or upset. Rather than lovingly listen to women, men tend to take a woman's negetive feelings personally as directed toward them and become angry. Thus she feels as though she must become someone other than who she is, someone perfect, to merit his love.

A third form of abuse is shown when men will often attempt to debate a woman, to wear her down, to prove that he's right. She feels, however, that he's a bully who's not interested in her viewpoint.

A fourth way to display abuse is when men either do not to respond to a woman's desire for conversation or listen out of one ear while thinking about or doing something else. This makes a woman feel ignored, that her husband doesn't really care about her or her or how she feels.

There is not a man alive today who will not abuse a woman in some way, whether passively or actively, just as there is no woman who will not abuse a man. Proverbs 20:9 says: "Who can say, 'I have kept my heart pure; I am clean and without sin?'" That's the result of the judgment in Genesis 3:15 and the way life will be for both men and women on planet earth. While this in no way condones or excuses wrongful action, it does help women to understand men. Most men locate somewhere between the two extremes of dominance and passivity with the majority opting for passive dominance. Wherever they land, they will be guilty of some of the above wrongs that result in abuse.

THE TRAGEDY

The tragedy is that just as the woman's self-protective attempts to control the man never work, neither does the man's self-protective dominance over the woman. Both attempts are the result of the Fall, not God's creative design, and both are abusive toward the other partner. God refuses to condone or honor either behavior.

When a man dominates a woman, whether actively or passively, to gain a sense of competence in his relationship with her, it's comparable to his trying to cover a gaping wound in his side with a band-aid. Ultimately it never works for several reasons. First, he's not properly relating to his wife in that he's not completing her according to God's design. In Genesis 2, God designed the man to be a servant leader to his wife, and He has given him both the authority to exercise leadership and the responsibility that comes with that authority. The natural result is the deep authentic relationship and rich intimacy described at the end of Genesis 2: "The man and his wife were both naked and they felt no shame." They were totally open with each other. There was no fear of vulnerability.

The tragedy is that just as the woman's self-protective attempts to control the man never work, neither does the man's self-protective dominance of the woman.

Since the Fall, all that has changed. Adam and Eve forfeited their relationship to be like God. Now to get his way and experience a sense of competence in their relationship, a man will dominate a woman in some way that results in either a mild or an extreme form of abuse. While domination may result in some feelings of adequacy on his part, it won't work. He will find his competence only in the Lord, not in dominating his wife (2 Cor. 3:4–6). Her response to protect herself will be to redouble her efforts to control him, so both lose.

Second, his maleness is frustrated. When he spends a certain amount of his time dominating his wife, and she spends her time controlling him, both frustrate their sexuality. Since God didn't design them to function this way, they will rarely experience what God intended for them in the marriage. Rather than fulfillment, they'll experience frustration.

His frustration has a lot to do with his feelings of inadequacy in their relationship. He'll handle his frustration and the pain it brings by moving toward those areas where he perceives that he's competent. Therefore, he will pour himself into his work, sports, hobbies, the television, yard work, the church, and so on. (She usually pours herself into her kids.) While these are not wrong in themselves, they have become his addictions to soothe the pain of his bruised male ego.

At the same time, he will move away from those areas of perceived incompetence. He may feel inadequate to relate well to his wife, children, other people, and so on. This is where he's weak. But rather than trying to grow stronger, he'll retreat instead to his areas of perceived competence. There he finds safety, security, and pain relief. As he pursues his areas of adequacy, he begins to feel competent again and good about himself. So he tells himself that everything must be okay because he feels good again. To the contrary, he has assumed the position of the proverbial ostrich, burying his head in his personal safety zone (his perceived competencies) while he has exposed his flank.

Third, his domination of his wife is self-defeating. His attempts to control her only add fuel to the relational fire. She as a responder will respond by attempting all the more to control him to protect herself from him. When this happens, he will try even harder to dominate her to protect himself from her. This becomes a vicious cycle (fig. 2). The woman says to herself: "I must take control of this relationship to protect myself (and possibly her family)," so she becomes strong and proactive. The man feels threatened. He's not quite sure what to do in this situation that signals that he may be out of his league and worse, that he's dreadfully incompetent. So he does what comes naturally; he abuses her by backing away from any emotional involvement with her. He may actively abuse her emotionally or physically by attacking her verbally or beating her. Or he may passively abuse her through ignoring her. Either way, he's abandoned her emotionally.

The woman feels the deep pain of his abandonment and tries even harder to take control of the situation. After all, what is she to do? She can't just sit around and watch her world fall apart. This results in even more pain for him, so he punishes her by retreating even further from her. Consequently, both feel a gnawing emptiness and a growing, overwhelming sense of pain. They both begin to realize that it's painful, very painful, to be in a relationship with this person, and eventually this leads to the death of their relationship.

DOMINANCE-CONTROL CYCLE

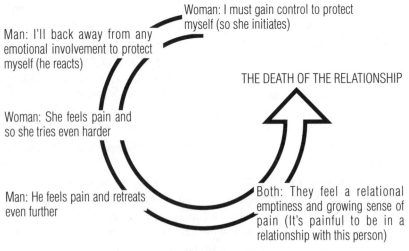

Woman: I must gain control to protect myself (so she initiates)

Man: I'll back away from any emotional involvement to protect myself (he reacts)

THE DEATH OF THE RELATIONSHIP

Woman: She feels pain and so she tries even harder

Man: He feels pain and retreats even further

Both: They feel a relational emptiness and growing sense of pain (It's painful to be in a relationship with this person)

(Figure 2)

THE REDEMPTIVE SOLUTION FOR THE MAN

God designed the man to be the primary leader in his relationship with his wife. That's how God wants him to complete her. But due to the Fall he'll attempt to dominate her instead (Gen. 3:16). The critical question is: What can he do about his propensity to abuse the woman? Is there any hope for him in Christ? What difference does Christ make in the relationship? What has Christ accomplished that could help a man to relate properly and in a godly way to his wife and break the vicious cycle that will in time cause the ultimate death of their relationship?

The answer is that Christ—the New Adam—makes all the difference. He's the only hope for men and their relationships. The solution for the man, as for the woman, is a redemptive relationship as predicted in Genesis 3:15 based on the Cross of Christ. The woman's seed (Christ) will bruise the serpent's head at the Cross, making it possible not only for a man and women to be reconciled to God, but to break the vicious cycle of mutual abuse predicted in Genesis 3:16.

The primary function for the man in his relationship with the woman is that of leader. The New Testament, however, emphasizes a redemptive element to his role. He is to be the loving leader in his marriage.

Whereas the Old Testament emphasized that the woman wonderfully complements her husband as his helper in their relationship, the New Testament emphasizes the element of submission. Her redemptive function is that of submissive helper. The primary function for the man in his relationship with the woman is that of a leader (Gen. 2–3 and 1 Cor. 11). The New Testament, however, emphasizes a redemptive element to his role. He is to be the loving leader in his marriage. But what does it mean for a man to love his wife? How is he to love her? Why should he love her? In Ephesians 5:25–33 Paul answers these questions and covers the what, how, why of the man's loving leadership of his wife.

The Man Is to Love His Wife

As the leader in the husband-wife relationship, the man is responsible to serve, not dominate, his wife. Biblical leadership is not dominance. The kind of leadership that characterized the pagans in Christ's time was dominance—the arbitrary flexing of one's authoritative muscle to lord it over people (Matt. 20:25). Christ teaches that this must not be among Christians, that Christian leadership is servant leadership as modeled by the incarnate Christ who came "not to be served, but to serve, and to give his life as a ransom for many" (Matt. 20:26–28). Christ's leadership was characterized by service that resulted in sacrifice.

In Ephesians 5:22–24 Paul directed wives to submit to their husbands. Just in case the man should not understand or interpret this as allowing him to do what comes naturally —to dominate her—Paul adds Ephesians 5:25–32 and specifically directs husbands in verse 25 to love their wives. In Ephesians 5:25 and other passages such as verses 28, 33, and Colossians 3:19, Paul reiterates the need and responsibility for men to love their wives. The idea is that the man's servant leadership is to be a loving leadership. His relationship to her throughout their marriage is to be a loving relationship. Headship is loving leadership; it's never to be equated with domination. Headship gives the man the authority, and thus the responsibility, to be the primary leader in the husband-wife relationship. But it isn't the authority to flex one's muscle or dominate the woman. God made the man the head, or responsible leader, in Genesis 2 (1 Cor. 11:7–9), but domination entered the picture after the Fall in Genesis 3 (Gen. 3:16). Ephesians 5:25–33 serves to add the all important element of love to the man's leadership.

Paul reiterates the need and responsibility for men to love their wives. The idea is that the man's servant leadership is to be a loving leadership. His relationship throughout their marriage is to be a loving relationship.

When a man obeys Scripture and loves his wife, he begins to feel competent in the relationship. The Fall has left him thinking that to be competent as a man he must dominate and control her. She responds to his domination by attempting to control him instead. He compensates by redoubling his efforts, and as Genesis 3:16 says, "he will rule over you." These actions and reactions only serve to drive a wedge between husband and wife that gradually worsens over the life of the relationship—they aid and abet the vicious cycle described above. Often, both withhold their love to punish the other partner. When a woman feels unloved, she feels unimportant and, in turn, she doesn't appreciate things that her husband might attempt to do for her. Her failure to appreciate him only heightens his feelings of inadequacy. A husband's loving leadership is the solution to his feelings of incompetence in their marriage. When a husband loves his wife, it makes it much easier for her to be submissive, not rebellious, to his leadership, and this brings him a sense of male competence.

The man's loving leadership is also the solution to breaking the vicious cycle of her control and his emotional distancing. When one of the partners interrupts the cycle and begins to function in the relationship according to his or her God-designed role, there is no guarantee that the other will respond, but the chances improve dramatically, especially if it's the man who initiates breaking the cycle. I argue the latter from the fact that he's the responsible point person. When he initiates and functions as God has designed him, I believe that it's easier for the woman to respond than vice versa. This is why God places so much responsibility for the relationship on the man and not the woman.

The Man Is to Love His Wife as Christ Loves His Church

How is a man to love his wife? Paul answers this question in the rest of Ephesians 5:25–33 where he says: "Husbands love your wives, just as Christ loved the church. . . ." But what does that mean? How did Christ love the church? It's interesting that Paul takes time to explain to the man what his love for his wife is supposed to look like. One can almost anticipate how a man who reads this passage might respond. Most wouldn't understand what Paul was talking about. Men tend to be very uncomfortable when they need or are asked to do something, and they don't know precisely what to do (it's the male competency thing again). So Paul spells it out for the man. He directs men to love their wives in two primary ways—sacrificially and as themselves.

A Man Is to Love His Wife Sacrificially. First, Paul directs men to love their wives: "just as Christ loved the church and gave himself up for her." The standard for a man's love is the Savior's love for His bride, the church. Men are to love their wives as Christ loved them and all other Christians who make up the church—the bride of Christ. But that sounds rather vague and general. The key phrase in the directive is his giving himself up for her. This characterizes the man's love as sacrificial. Paul is saying that a man's love for his wife is to be sacrificial. His point is that if a man is going to love his wife as Christ loved the church, he's got to make some sacrifices for her as Christ did for us.

The tendency is for men to focus on themselves and their needs, and they forget their families, who have needs as well. For example, men mistakenly believe that by pouring themselves into their work that they're loving their wives and families because they're providing for their primary physical needs. She begins to feel lonely and neglected, and so she asks: "Do you love me?" He responds, "Of course I love you, why do you think I work so hard?" While there is some truth to his response, the reality is that he's also working hard because it makes him feel more adequate as a man. He's pursuing an area of perceived competence that he interprets as loving his wife. Loving her, however, should result in her not feeling all alone and abandoned.

*One primary sacrifice is for him to listen to her,
especially her feelings.*

How does a man love his wife sacrificially? What are some of the sacrifices that he'll need to make for her? One primary sacrifice is for him to listen to her, especially her feelings. While Adam's primary mistake in Genesis 3 is that he was listening to the woman when he should have been leading her (v. 17), men must not construe this to mean that a man is never to listen to his wife. Leading involves listening, and loving leadership involves loving listening. He needs to listen to find out what her needs are. Adam's problem is that he listened but failed to take action. He became passive when things went bad.

When a man lovingly listens to a woman as a fellow image-bearer, several important things take place for her. He validates and honors her worth as a person so that she feels esteemed, secure, and respected as a woman. She also senses that he cares about her feelings and, even more, that he understands her, whether he actually does or not.

So many men don't realize that these things are very important to a woman. Instead of listening, especially when she's upset, he thinks he's being loving when he attempts to solve her problems or minimizes their importance. He seeks closure, whereas she seeks openness. He says, "You have a problem, let me fix it for you." Or he says, "It's not as bad as you think."

Mr. Fix-it's desire for closure is simply another way of gaining a sense of competence, only at her expense (he feels amazingly good about himself when he thinks he's solved her problem). The result is devastating for a woman. Instead of feeling loved, she feels judged, minimized, and unappreciated. She's not necessarily looking for a quick fix, but for a listening ear that says she's been heard and understood. And who is he to say: "It's not as bad as you think"? How does he know, especially if he's not taken the time to listen? Proverbs 18:13 warns men: "He who answers before listening—that is his folly and his shame." In all this he signals that it's not safe for her to be herself while he's around.

Another sacrifice that shows a man's love for his wife affects his time. He needs to devote more time and energy to her. Any relationship takes time, especially that between a man and a woman. A man's tendency is to use his time for himself. This is not as true at the beginning of the relationship. To woo and win his bride, he's willing to set some time aside for her. But after they're married and as he finds perceived areas of competence, his temptation will be to pour his time into those things, not his wife. This robs both him and his wife of the time that they desperately need together to develop their relationship.

Another sacrifice that shows a man's love for his wife affects his time. He needs to devote more time and energy to her.

Most men are willing to give their wives some time. Giving unscheduled time, however, is not always a priority. Men tend to operate on a schedule, and like to work their wives into that schedule. She says: "We need some time together" which being interpreted means, "I need some time with you." As he pulls out his calendar, he responds: "I have worked you into my schedule later this evening." This is a real turn off for her, and signals that she's not a priority. She wants access to his time whenever she needs it.

It's not necessarily wrong for a man to operate with a calendar in hand. And it's not wrong for him to schedule time with his wife. He has to go to work and doesn't need numerous interruptions. The latter can prove to be an unnecessary distraction. They can plan to spend time together in the evenings at home. It's imperative that they understand the other's needs. She should feel free to call him and interrupt his schedule when it's important, and she needs to be enough of a priority that he stops what he's doing for her when she really needs him.

A third sacrifice that expresses a man's love is his willingness to do lots of little things for his wife. Whether they'll admit it, men and women keep score in their relationships. Men assume that when they do something big for their wives, such as take her away for a weekend or buy her a car, they score more points than when they take her out to eat, buy her flowers, or take her to a movie. But that's not true. It's the little things that make the big difference. One writer says: "A man doesn't realize that to a woman the little things are just as important as the big things. In other words, to a woman, a single rose gets as many points as paying the rent on time. Without understanding this basic difference in score keeping, men and women are continually frustrated and disappointed in their relationships."[2]

A third sacrifice that expresses a man's love is his willingness to do lots of little things for his wife.

The implication is that a husband must be willing to set aside the time to do many little things for his wife. He must ask: What can I do today that will make life a little bit easier for this woman? This includes such acts as praying with her, regular hugs and kisses, focused listening—especially when she's upset—occasional flowers, cleaning the bathroom, washing and vacuuming her car, respecting her opinion on topics, loading the dishwasher and washing the plates and silverware, discussing spiritual truth, keeping her informed, getting the kids dressed, taking out the trash, encouraging her, changing diapers, not channel surfing, running errands for her, ironing, recognizing when she's had a hard day, vacuuming the house, noticing what she's wearing, complimenting her appearance, leaving her love notes, getting her to church on time, not trying to fix her or solve her problems, watching the kids so she can have some free time alone, and others.

Since these things take some time and some thought, the woman will appreciate them greatly. They signal to her that he understands that she's not there to be a maid and meet his personal needs. She realizes that she is a priority in the man's life and that he's been thinking about her and loves her or he wouldn't bother. There are some things that are very difficult for a man to do. It might be going shopping with his wife or stopping to say hello and socializing with the girls at an all-ladies' event in the home. What constitutes unpleasant tasks varies from man to man. Regardless, a wife notices and appreciates it when a man does these difficult things just to be with her or help her.

A Man Is to Love His Wife as He Loves Himself. The second primary way a man is to love his wife is to love her as himself. In Ephesians 5:28 Paul writes: "In this same way, husbands ought to love their wives as their own bodies. He who loves his wife loves himself." On the surface this appears rather narcissistic. While one must be careful and not go overboard into narcissism, there is a proper self-love. Moses calls for it in Leviticus 19:18, and Jesus commands it in Matthew 19:19. Paul describes it in verse 29: "After all, no one ever hated his own body, but he feeds and cares for it, just as Christ does the church." It's imperative that a man take the responsibility to feed and take care of himself. This includes washing his body, eating regularly, maintaining a proper diet, and protecting himself from harm by wearing proper clothing and avoiding dangerous situations.

When a man marries a woman, he assumes another responsibility besides himself. As he loves his own body, now he loves his wife because the two have become one flesh (v. 31). What he does for himself, he is responsible to do for his wife. These include the big things in life. I've stated above that a man loves a woman sacrificially when he carves time out of his busy schedule to do the little things for her that score as many points in the long term as the big things. Paul seems to be stressing the importance of the big things. Big things are important as well as necessary. It's the old adage of missing the forest because of all the trees. A man can get caught up in doing the little things and somehow miss or ignore the big things that also display his love for her.

What are some of these big things? They are the basics of life such as feeding and taking care of the woman. A man is loving and responsible when he provides the basics for her as he would for himself. While she may work, he will need to hold down a regular job that provides the finances to satisfy their needs and not just their wants. Maintaining a certain lifestyle has become problematic for many couples across America. Many are image conscious and, with easy credit, tend to spend more than they earn to provide for their wants and to maintain what for them is an exorbitant lifestyle. A man loves his wife when he holds them to their budget.

There are some other big things. One is his providing a roof over their head. They must have a place to live. Another is a proper diet. They need to eat healthy, nourishing food to protect and maintain good health. A third is good medical and dental care to protect them in case of disease and bodily injury. A fourth is purchasing and wearing the proper clothing. A fifth is providing adequate means of transportation. Most will own at least one car. A woman feels loved when a man makes sure that their vehicle is always in proper working order so that she's not left stranded on some roadside. When a man is single, he may often ignore these big things because they aren't as important to him as his work and other activities. He always seems to get by. When he marries, however, and takes on the responsibility of a wife, they are an important part of his love for her.

A woman feels loved by a man when he remembers and does the little things suggested above. She may or may not feel as loved when he provides the big or basic things for her. But she should realize that they are as important as the little things and often make the little things possible. She should show her appreciation for his provision of the big things as well as the little things and realize that they are a legitimate way for him to display his love and affection for her. The problem, of course, is when he depends only on the big things as the means of expressing his love and ignores the smaller acts of love.

The Man Is to Love His Wife Because It Benefits Her. It would seem strange to have to ask why a man should love his wife. Yet Paul answers this question in Ephesians 5:26–27. The answer is that it benefits her spiritually. God has appointed the man as the loving leader who carries the primary responsibility for their relationship. A part of his responsibility is the spiritual side of their relationship. In far too many families, the woman has taken the responsibility for her and her family's spiritual development. Men have wrongly divorced manhood and spirituality, and promptly left spirituality in the hands of their wives. This is not to be in the Christian family.

The husband's love for his wife illustrates and demonstrates to her Christ's love for his church of which she's a vital part.

In verses 26–27 Paul writes that the purpose of Christ's death was both positive and negative with the church. His death was positive in that he died to make her holy (v. 26). It was negative in that he died so that his church could be without stain or wrinkle (v. 27). The implication is that while a man cannot die for his wife as Christ did, resulting in the forgiveness of her sins, he can benefit her spiritually by loving her sacrificially. The husband's sacrificial love for his wife illustrates and demonstrates to her Christ's love for his church of which she's a vital part. This love will motivate her, in turn, to love and appreciate all that Christ has done for her and will foster her desire for maturity in Christ. Consequently, a man is most like Christ in his marriage when he lovingly leads his wife.

DISCUSSION QUESTIONS

For Men

1. Do you believe that as a man you tend to dominate women? If no, how do you explain Genesis 3:16? If yes, explain. What is it that you do that is dominating?

2. Do you ever wrestle as a man with feelings of inadequacy? Has there ever been a major time in your life when you failed as Moses did in Exodus 2, and you've not been able to recover from it? If yes, what do you plan to do about it? Should you seek professional help? If yes, will you? According to 2 Corinthians 3:4–6, where should you look for your competence and feelings of confidence?

3. Do you feel competent in your present occupation? Do you feel adequate in your relationship with women? If you're married, do you feel competent in your marriage? If yes, why? If no, why not? Describe any feelings of inadequacy.

4. Do you ever fear failure? When? Where? How do you explain your fear according to Genesis 3? Do you ever measure your worth by your performance, especially in your work? How might a fear of failure affect your relationship with a woman? Do the women you're in contact with seem to understand a man's fear of failure? How has this affected you and your comfort with your sexuality?

5. A man's fear of incompetence in his relationship with a woman naturally leads to a self-protective dominance. Have you found yourself drifting toward either of the two extremes of dominance? Do you have a tendency toward being harsh and overbearing or weak and impotent? Have you ever found yourself minimizing a woman's feelings? Do you carefully listen to your wife when she's feeling upset? If no, why not? Do you have a tendency to argue with your wife until she gives in? How well do you listen to your wife in general? Have you ever viewed these practices as a form of abuse?

6. In your experience, has dominating your wife ever worked in the sense that it has improved your relationship? Why? Has dominating your wife ever frustrated you and left you feeling inadequate as a male? The natural tendency for most men is to move toward their areas of perceived competence. Do you do this? What are those areas where you feel most competent? While there may be nothing wrong with any of those things in themselves, have you ever viewed them as addictions? Why or why not? Do you believe that you and your wife are caught up in a vicious dominance-control cycle? If yes, then where are you in that cycle?

7. If you're married, do you believe that you really love your wife? Why or why not? Can you possibly love your wife as Christ loves the church? Do you love your wife sacrificially? How do

you know? What kinds of sacrifices do you make for your wife? What kinds of sacrifices are you willing to make? How much time do you set aside for your wife? What are some of the little things that you do for her? How does she respond? What are some little things that you don't presently do but would like to do?

8. Do you love your wife as you love yourself? Why or why not? What are some of the big things that you do for her? How do they express your love for her? Are they as important to her as the little things? How do you know? Have you ever asked her? What are some big things that you should be doing for her?

9. Do you see yourself as playing an important role in the spiritual nurturing of your wife? Why or why not? Who is responsible for the spiritual life of your family, you or your wife? Why? How does being the spiritual leader in your home affect your wife?

Notes

1. Bill Ordine, "Suicide looms most heavily over older white men," *The Dallas Morning News,* May 4, 1995, p. 1C.

2. John Gray, *Men Are from Mars, Women Are from Venus* (New York, N.Y.: HarperCollins Publishers, 1992), p. 178.

Epilogue
A Look into the Future

The sleek Boeing 747 roared down the broad concrete runway, then climbed quickly into the partly cloudy sky over the Dallas-Fort Worth Airport. Carol and Randy were momentarily blinded by the bright sun as they strained to observe the Dallas skyline through the plane's windows. Once the large jet had leveled off at around 32,000 feet over eastern New Mexico, the captain announced that he would turn off the Fasten Your Seat Belts sign, but asked that all passengers remain in their seats for the present because there was some reported turbulence over New Mexico due to weather conditions. They were on their way again to the beautiful, sandy beaches and clear, blue-green waters of Honolulu, Hawaii, to celebrate their tenth wedding anniversary.

Whereas approximately half of American couples end their marriages in divorce, Randy and Carol are still together. Though neither would describe their relationship as all smooth sailing, they're relatively happy and still very much in love. On the one hand, several things have changed for them. They now have a six-year-old daughter, Karen, and a two-year-old son, Kevin. While Randy continues to work full time, Carol has shifted to working part-time so that she can be at home more for her kids.

On the other hand, some things haven't changed. They still attend and are very active at Fellowship Community Church, and occasionally spend some time with Dr. Steve Smith, who is still a counselor on staff at the church. His biblical counseling and coaching earlier in their marriage has proved to be very beneficial. They feel that they know where the mines are hidden in their relational field and how to defuse or work around them.

This doesn't mean, however, that they don't continue to struggle. There are still times in their marriage when she attempts to control him, and he responds by dominating her. After all, that's the way life will be for a man and a woman on planet earth according to Genesis 3. While Scripture offers wise counsel that will help them to relate better, there are no magical formulas one can follow or potions one can drink that will result in the perfect marriage. Thousands of years after the Garden, Satan is still busy doing everything in his power to pull off a heavenly coup, and he's convinced that targeting the family is a critical part of his strategy. This means that the most mature marriages will at times struggle deeply, experience intense pain, and walk through the valley of the shadow of death. Growth in God's grace and increasing spiritual maturity doesn't necessarily correlate with a decrease in life's troubles.

To a great degree, life remains a mystery. I believe that God planned it that way. Otherwise, what reason would we have to cling to him and trust him for our relationships as well as our very lives. If we could figure God out, then perhaps we could remove some of the mystery that life holds for us. But then He would no longer be God.

What does God expect, therefore, of us? What does he want us to do? I'm convinced that he wants us to obey and trust him in spite of our circumstances, whether good or bad. In 1 Samuel 15:22 God's prophet asks Saul: "Does the Lord delight in burnt offerings and sacrifices as much as in obeying the voice of the Lord? To obey is better than sacrifice, and to heed is better than the fat of rams." In John 14:15 Jesus says to his disciples: "If you love me, you will obey what I command."

God also delights in us when we trust him in the difficult times. In John 14:1 the Savior says to his disciples: "Do not let your hearts be troubled. Trust in God; trust also in me." In the wisdom teaching of Proverbs 3:5–6 the writer advises: "Trust in the Lord with all your heart and lean not on your own understanding; in all your ways acknowledge him, and he will make your paths straight."

When most men and women get married, especially the first time, their expectations of one another and their vision of their lives together are unrealistic. Their relational recipe consists of living together happily ever after. Genesis 3 adds a heaping cup of hard times and pain and disillusionment to the batter. Regardless, I believe that God wants men and women to obey his instructions regarding their relationships and trust him for them during the worst of times as well as the best of times. That is what it means to be an authentic man or women.

Authentic men work hard at treating their wives with respect as equal image-bearers. They understand and accept their roles as primary servant leaders in their marriages and trust God the Holy Spirit to help them not to abuse but love their wives as Christ loved his church. In this way they mirror God's image as the Spirit produces the very character of Christ in their lives (Gal. 4:19; 5:22–23). Theirs is not a problem-free marriage. When they fail, which is often, they don't walk away from their responsibilities even though they are tempted to. While they don't understand life which is most frightening, they refuse to throw in the towel. Instead, they're still in the ring, trusting God as best they can (sometimes blindly) for their circumstances.

Authentic women work hard at embracing their roles as supportive helpers and trust the Spirit to help them submit to, rather than control, their husbands. In this way they, too, mirror God's image. This doesn't mean that they don't mess up along the way; they do, and it happens almost daily. This can be very disconcerting and frustrating. Yet they continue to function in spite of their temptations and difficulties. They haven't arrived yet but seek to trust and obey Christ as best they can in their growing passion for Him.